Absolutely You!

Anita Sechesky

Absolutely You!

Library and Archives Canada Cataloguing in Publication

Sechesky, Anita, author
   Absolutely you : overcome self-limitations and unleash your full potential! / Anita Sechesky.

ISBN 978-1-897453-46-9 (pbk.)

   1. Self-actualization (Psychology) in women. 2. Self-control. I. Title.

BF637.S4S426 2014   158.1082   C2014-906513-2

Cover design/realization Donovan Davie: 519-501-2375
Cover photograph courtesy Shutterstock

First Edition. 144 pages. All rights reserved.
Published October 15, 2014
Manor House Publishing Inc.
www.manor-house.biz (905) 648-2193

We acknowledge the financial support of the Government of Canada through the Canada Book Fund (CBF) for this project.

By the same bestselling author: *Living Without Limitations - 30 Mentors To Rock Your World; Living Without Limitations - 30 Stories To Heal Your World* and *#Love – A New Generation of Hope*

Note: The content contained within this book *Absolutely You!* does not substitute any form of professional counsel. The information provided does not constitute professional or legal advice and the author assumes no liability in this regard. The author is merely providing her personal viewpoints and advice in hopes the reader will derive helpful benefit from this and assess/utilize said information in a responsible manner.

TABLE OF CONTENTS

FOREWORD

I've known Anita several years, after we first met at a Body Esteem workshop. As time passed, we realized our friendship was deeper on a spiritual level and there are parallels in our lives that have strengthened our bond as friends and confidants. Anita's strong intuition, analytical ability, and compassion have made her one of the most sought-after life coaches and motivational speakers today.

Anita's talents are evident in her collaborative efforts with co-authors, accessible world-wide in the best-selling books, *Living Without Limitations – 30 Mentors to Heal Your World* and *Living Without Limitations – 30 Stories to Heal Your World.* I'm honoured to be chosen by Anita to write the foreword in her first solo book, *Absolutely You!*

Anita has powerfully impacted my life as a great friend and life coach during times of my feeling "stuck" in life situations. And there are many others out there who have fallen into despair or become confused by unexpected life alternating moments. Anita's book sheds light into those moments of darkness. The chapters are engaging reminders for daily living without limitations.

When we are born, we are taught rules created by the blueprints of our society. "Boys don't cry," or "Girls are nice." What happens to some of us is that we create a rigid self-concept that ultimately affects our self esteem, which is the core value we place on ourselves based on how we self identity. Anita's book, offers a chance to reset thought patterns by first reconnecting back to our true selves though self love. Once that reconnection is in place we are at peace with ourselves and can truly love others.

Absolutely You! has 22 self affirming chapters to release our mind's limitations by helping us to step into our place of power by reinforcing that we are valuable, worthwhile, sexy, beautiful, capable, confident, intelligent, loveable, ambitious, successful, graceful, and forgiving. Women, traditionally, are socialized to nurture and give in to the needs of others at their expense. But women can become resentful because their own emotional needs are not met. As a result, many women internalize their anger and frustration and turn to unhealthy behaviors – drinking, overeating, gossiping – to find escape or comfort, at great cost to their mental and emotional health.

Depression and anxiety are at all time highs in society because women are not giving themselves permission to be happy. Every chapter in this book allows the reader to examine different life challenges with clear, simple, practical ways of redirecting their thoughts towards personal empowerment.

Anita has set out a wealth of wisdom and knowledge as if she is sitting right there with you discussing these topics and issues that all of us women face depending on where we are at any moment in our busy lives. This book will allow women of all ages to get a better understanding of situations they're facing. I believe it will be a resource for women for years to come because of the depth of each chapter and how easily one can relate to it as a woman.

Many of the topics Anita discusses are things we would talk about with our girlfriends, sisters, mothers, and daughters. I really enjoyed reading this book and look forward to reading it again as it is packed with so many resources. I know I will get something different out of it each time I read it. This powerful book is a guide to recharging your emotional and spiritual batteries in order to be healthy, happy, and a whole woman.

- **Nikki Clarke**, Teacher, Producer/Host of Nikki Clarke Show, Founder of Nikki Clarke Network, 24 hour online T.V. network

DEDICATION / ACKNOWLEDGEMENTS

It is with great pleasure that I take this time to acknowledge the people who have stood by, supported, and loved me for who I have become today. I am so grateful to God for this blanket of love that continually surrounds me and lifts me up. These individuals have contributed to the woman that I am and it is because of their unconditional love towards me that has inspired and supported my dream to do more for others. Their love has helped me to grow emotionally through my own life experiences so that I can assist others to do the same.

I would like to now take this opportunity to acknowledge Stephen, the love of my life for believing in me and my desire to always strive for greater purpose in all that I do. Your unconditional love and friendship have inspired me in this journey. Thank you for being who you are to me and our boys.

To my eldest son Nathaniel: Thank you for being such an amazing son. I love you more and more each day. You inspire me and make me so proud to be your mother. You are an intelligent, kind and loving individual. I adore your sense of humour and appreciate all the special gifts God has blessed you with to appreciate knowledge and seek wisdom in all your ways. Always remember what an amazing gift from God you are, to not only your family, but also to those around you. Never give up on your dreams. You were a success from the day you were born. I believe in you.

To Samuel: Thank you, my darling son for the joy that you bring to Mommy. I love your curiosity as a child, always fixing and taking things apart. You have the mind of a genius with so much potential. The world is unfolding before your very eyes. You never cease to amaze me with your growing wisdom and skills. God has great plans for you. Success is in every step that you take. I'm so proud to call you "My darling little boy." I believe in you.

To my beautiful Mother Jean Seergobin: Thank you for always encouraging me to see the beauty in the world around me and encouraging me to never give up, you are my best friend mom and I love you dearly. To my distinguished Father, Jetty Seergobin: Thank you for showing me how to never be discouraged in life but to carry on despite whatever circumstances I may be facing in life. Mom and Dad: I love you both so much, because of your love for me. I have never given up on doing more for the greater good. You each have inspired me to be a better person and look past my own fears, failures and the criticisms of others. I am so blessed to have you as my parents. May God bless us all with long and healthy lives together as a family. I love you Mom and Dad.

To my brother Trevor Seergobin: Thank you for allowing me the room to grow professionally and chase my dreams, including becoming an International Best Selling Author. Your continued support, encouragement and praise makes me think of you more as my big brother and I'm so proud to call you my brother. I believe in you too!

For all the people who've been part of my life and supported my dreams and ambitions, thank you for being the wonderful friends, colleagues and family that you are to me. I love and appreciate each of you for who you are.

I'd also like to give an unusual appreciation to those who have caused me heartache, disappointments and pain. Because of you, I never gave up in life, it was the hardships that you put me through that made me strive harder to believe in unconditional love that is lacking in this world. Two wrongs never make a right. I forgive.

- Anita Sechesky

INTRODUCTION

As I reflect on the moments that I have been blessed with, never in a million years would I have thought that my words could touch so many people around the world. I thank you dear readers for supporting and following me through my previous international best-selling books: *Living Without Limitations – 30 Mentors to Rock Your World*, *Living Without Limitations – 30 Stories to Heal Your World* as well as my most recent anthology project *#Love – A New Generation of Hope.*

My company, Anita Sechesky – Living Without Limitations, is based on my value of integrity to bring hope, inspiration, and empowerment to all who may have endured what I have, or even worse. I strive to help people recognize that no one has the right, no matter who they are, to belittle, degrade or destroy another's dreams. As a nurse, I've witnessed many patients whose dreams were never fully lived and sadly perished with them.

As a Life Coach, I have helped people who cannot see their own self-worth, have lost hope and settled, or lost self confidence because no one believed in them. I understand that kind of damage and want to show people how the power of communication can be used effectively. At some point everyone has to realize that they cannot allow others to continue limiting and degrading them.

I strongly believe every person deserves to be given the opportunity to reach higher, stand taller, and surpass their own expectations and goals. What does your life look like? Does your personal life need a new outlook or game plan? Then I know you will gain insight from reading this book.

Resilience is something we each carry within ourselves, but not until we are tested do we recognize how much we can accomplish in our lives. This opportunity to present a book that brings hope and inspiration on so many levels is yet just another part of my childhood dream to help many.

Absolutely You! encapsulates so much of what I believe in and stand for, not just as a woman but as a person of priceless value. Every woman is beautiful and has a voice to be heard. She needs to allow herself the opportunity to hear her voice speak loud and clear. It's time that women appreciate that just as we are all unique, we also have the same kind of emotions and dreams in life. There's nothing that a woman cannot do if she puts her mind to it. This book is very special to me as it is a powerhouse of wisdom and knowledge that I have gained over the years. The collection of thoughts that I share within these pages is meant for you to be empowered and motivated as the beautiful soul that you are. If it inspires you in any way to live the life that you have been dreaming of, then this book has fulfilled its purpose.

A change to a positive perspective is a gift that only you can give to yourself. With that in mind you will see anything is possible! Your dreams can come true. Just start to believe and increase your faith in yourself and a higher power, which I choose to call God my Heavenly Father. You will finally start to see that the sky is the limit.

My desire for you, as you read this book, is to find the inspiration you are looking for to make the positive changes in your life. Don't let your fears live any longer. Give your dreams the life they deserve to live victoriously through you. This book is not intended to replace the counsel of a Psychologist or Therapist, but to only give the reader insight into areas that may need encouragement as a female in all areas of your life.

1 Limitations are NOT Sexy

When a girl is born, she's a princess full of expectations and excitement. Yet so many women are not living the life of their dreams. This is a result of limitations being formed in their lives from early childhood carrying a myriad of gender specific traits regardless of geographical or cultural backgrounds.

Often times, women respond as society would expect them to with no recourse for motivating bruised egos, broken hearts, damaged emotions, and lost ambitions.

If you desire to become the woman you long to be, then you have to let the Princess go to the Ball! You have to allow yourself to become all that you were created to be as a passionate female. Embrace your femininity and all your shortcomings. Then learn how to empower yourself by not being confined to the limits that can block your dreams and ambitions. As a Life Coach, I help my female clients to take a closer look at how false perceptions can emotionally cripple and negatively affect the sexy and successful women they were born to be!

Let's take a closer look and learn how to identify the limitations and the negative energy that is attached to them. By doing so, you can save many relationships from ending prematurely. This new awareness will help a woman to embrace her opportunities to market, promote and become successful. Once these barriers are identified as characteristics and behaviours of how we interact with various individuals, the benefits are limitless. Recognizing that energy is movement and in order to see growth, you need more positive thought energy to continue moving forward or this downward heavy feeling of negativity will drain you. If it doesn't empower you or help you to be a confident person, then why are you keeping it around?

We attract many of these limitations into our lives at one point or another because we feel less than perfect, below average, not attractive, rich or smart enough. These kinds of thoughts become blocked energy, which attracts obstacles to your success. When you identify areas in your life where hidden traps have become part of your value system, then you can address it for what it is and send it back where it needs to go. Remove the blockages in your life and open doors of greater opportunities!

For anyone dealing with lack of motivation or low self-esteem, perceptions and attitudes are globally changing. Female entrepreneurs have stepped forward and overcome many of these boundaries successfully. If you are still struggling with memories of bad experiences growing up, embarrassing moments or hopelessness, you need to make a decision about what kind of life you really want to live. By keeping your positive energy flowing and addressing the things that are blocking your personal value you can prevent the limitations to your progress. This way you are allowing the creativity of your sexy genius to become fully alive within you and break off these labels and road blocks.

I encourage you to search within your heart to discover and identify the things that have caused stagnation and even sadness. You can still live a life without limitations that's productive and satisfying, but you need to first address these issues. If you are ready for this life, then it's time to start changing your perceptions now.

Here are some of the most common limitations I have seen women struggle with. Let's add some positive life lessons to *SEXY* things up!

1) **I'm not good enough** – Negative Limiting Belief

   Positive Life Lesson – **I am good enough!** Why believe someone else's opinion of your value? YOU are one of a kind. YOU are genuine and the real deal. YOU are an original masterpiece. You are confident and classy! You can do anything you set your mind to. You are a winner! Increase your value and believe in yourself. Let go and forgive all those, including yourself, for believing in less than you are. You ARE good enough!

2) **I'm not smart enough** – Negative Limiting Belief

   Positive Life Lesson – **I am a Sexy Genius!** Your creative intellect has been inspired from deep within your very soul. Speak to your universe and realize that you have all power and authority to overcome all limits of your intelligence. Keep learning, be open-minded and continually educate yourself in things that ignite your passion! Follow your heart and bring out your authentic self! Grade point averages and test scores do not determine your future outlook unless you allow them to, you Sexy genius!

3) **I'm not pretty enough** – Negative Limiting Belief

   Positive Life Lesson – **I am Beautiful and Sexy!** Do you really honestly believe the opinions of others; especially those who have no authority to give it unless you are allowing it? Maybe it's time to change your crew. The more you associate with people who look down on you or make you feel unworthy instead of your sexy self, the more you begin to believe them. Choose to believe that you are beautiful, pretty, and yes, even SEXY! Be adventurous and experiment with new looks and styles that compliment your body type. Trust the opinions of others and professionals. Do research in fashion magazines. Learn about colors and skin tones, fabrics and make-up. Embrace your femininity! Don't be shy and feel inadequate and don't ever let another person make you feel less than the Beautiful and Sexy woman that you already are!

4) **I can't do that** – Negative Limiting Belief

Positive Life Lesson – **I can do it!** You are intelligent, beautiful, creative, sensitive, and loving. Why can't you do what you want and be all that you want to be? If your intentions are pure and honest with integrity, there should be no limits to you finding a way. Make your life satisfying by living out your dreams. Don't let life pass you by with regrets. It's time to visualize yourself accomplishing your goals and ambitions. Once you see it in your visions, it will become so much easier to achieve. You can do it!

5) **I don't fit in** – Negative Limiting Belief

Positive Life Lesson – **I was born to STAND out!** Sometimes it's better to not fit in. Leaders are meant to stand out. Leaders don't look for confidence from others, they create their own self-confidence from within by being their authentic self. Make your mark by embracing who you are and establishing yourself as a woman of value. Love yourself more because you are your best friend. Let go of all hurtful and unpleasant memories. Free yourself from this painful trap! Only you can set yourself free! You're better than that. You've got what it takes, and you weren't made to fit in... you were born to stand out!

6) **I'm not what they want** – Negative Limiting Belief

Positive Life Lesson – **I am just what they're looking for!** Just because you came to some closed doors in your life doesn't mean the right open doors aren't there. Start believing for a better outcome. Let go of past failures. Let go of all fears of rejection. Be open-minded. Be excited. Be happy for the amazing opportunities coming your way. Envision it. Dream it. Taste it and talk about it. Attract the open doors into your life. You get to create your success first! You *are* what they want – you're just what they're looking for!

7) **I'll never find true love** – Negative Limiting Belief

Positive Life Lesson – **True love will find me!** Love is universal. Love makes the world go around. Love begins with you. How you feel is what you will attract. Are you looking for your knight in shining armour? Then love yourself more. Let go of fears and all past memories of failed relationships or stories you have heard. Stop these damaging emotional thoughts from draining you. Find yourself once again. Believe in love and love will find you when you least expect it. Appreciate who you are. Do more things that you enjoy. Be creative. Dream more and think of the life you want, go ahead and write your own fairytale life now! True Love will find you!

8) **Married Life is Boring** – Negative Limiting Belief

Positive Life Lesson – **Marriage is Passionate, Secure and Sexy!** Now that you have found your true Love, don't lose your Sexiness!!! Your life partner is your main support system and you need to include them in all the wonderful facets of who are. Dedication and attention to this relationship will directly affect your confidence and self-esteem. Many men and women get so comfortable with each other after marriage that they forget who they were when dating. Bring the Sexy back! You know what I mean. You had it and you know what to do about it! Marriage can be passionate, secure and sexy!

Can you see how easy it is to change your perceptions? If you are still struggling with any of these areas, then you are going to love my book. I am going to discuss each of these eight topics in depth and more as we move through the following pages. I want to help you identify what your passions are and focus more on it. As you become more enlightened and empowered you will find the confidence and inspiration you need to motivate yourself towards the life you desire. You can easily eliminate limitations and make all your dreams come true. As your intention becomes stronger, positive energy increases and frequencies are tuned in, therefore attracting the right timing for business opportunities, relationships, and clients. You can now be that magnet for the right people to come along side you, to love and support your vision and build your dreams with you. These are the people that you want to be there!

You were born a Princess but when you face your limitations, you become the Queen of your own Destiny!

Living beyond your Limitations is really SEXY!

Absolutely You Keys for Empowerment #1

Live each day with gratitude for the life you have and graciously welcome the gifts of health, healing and happiness into your world. Stop holding on to labels and negative mindsets as they're limitations in your way.

2 I am MORE than Good enough!

Yes, you are more than good enough! Why believe someone else's opinion of your value and self-worth as a woman? So many times in our lives we allow ourselves to be influenced and impacted by the attitudes and behaviours of people around us. In many cases, these very people don't even care or know us personally. Society has caused such complacency in the way that women look at themselves these days. Although we may have come a far way from the discrimination that our mothers once faced, there is still a stigma surrounding the powerful roles that women can attain as leaders in society. For instance, consider the reality that many women often struggle with having enough confidence that it doesn't rock the boat when it is needed to dissipate the negativity and criticisms that come their way.

As a female you are a powerful contributor to the population of humanity on this planet. The day you were born, the earth rejoiced because you are a new creation with the power of love within you. You are a gift to all that know you and you are perfectly created in the image of your creator. Your infinite greatness was unleashed into your life's journey and beyond. You are creating the future because you have the gift of procreation within your womb. You are strong and yet you are gentle. Each and every person that you encounter has only met you for who you are. There is no one else like you. The very choices that you make in life are different from those of others. Your experiences are unique to your chemistry. Every emotion that you feel is funded by the intricate connection of your cellular DNA. Your reactions are the response of life itself happening to you and around you. Although you have a choice to control your behaviours, unexpected situations can and do happen causing you to react in the most logical way that only you would. Because of these things, your individuality sets you apart. There is no one else like you. Even your fingerprints cannot lie but indeed tell this very story. What an amazing fact to know there is only one of you and you are one of kind. Original and true to the bone, sadly many people try so hard to become something they are not or even deny their own feelings to please others. If you've ever been guilty of this don't allow it to discourage you from becoming the person you are deep inside.

Everyone has role models in life and many times we become so complacent in who we actually are trying to become based on the expectations of others, our roles and responsibilities in our lives, that our persona becomes a façade that we carry around. I have come to understand in my own life and through the things I have seen in others that it is all just a normal part of our evolution to personal greatness and success. This may be the very reason why cosmetics are in such a high demand. Women are either trying to enhance what they are or cover it up. Also, with the increased trend of self-help books and training on the market, it is not difficult to understand why so many women may think they need improving or fixing. It really is a hodgepodge of societal expectations.

Think back to everything you've ever accomplished up to this point in your life. Do you remember taking your first baby-steps? Was there anyone criticizing which direction you were going in, or how many times you fell? Does it even matter now? Obviously you have what it takes to do what you want and accomplish it. I mean, how educated and knowledgeable were you when you were taking that first step, and yet you followed through and accomplished your goal successfully. Bravo! Not only can you walk now, but you can run. How's kicking that up a notch for you?

Many times we don't acknowledge our own small successes in life, and because of our lack of appreciation that this life has blessed us with we often forget how big they really are. Life is a journey of small steps with a big picture. You get to create your own masterpiece as the artist of your life. Do you think that any of the great masters of music and art listened to the opinions of others? Sure they may have mulled over quite a few critical comments but ultimately can you see how they allowed their passions to generate so much confidence within themselves that it was a bold step of faith on their parts to step out and be original in their styles? Imagine if they had allowed criticism to affect their final craftsmanship. Quite possibly their masterpieces may not have stood out and left the impact they did throughout the generations. By staying true to their passion and purpose in life, their personal impact and value increased tremendously over time.

So what's stopping you from becoming all that you want to be? Why are you allowing stuff to create a fear that's preventing you from becoming all that you are meant to be in this time of your life? I must say that anything not worthy of your greatness is not worthy of your attention. If it inspires and celebrates who you are, it's a keeper. But if it's the opposite then it could only mean one thing....Yes it's a fear and limitation, and definitely NOT sexy! I would like to ask you to be conscious of the emotions that are stirred up within you when contemplating your goals in life. Why does it have to be so difficult to move forward in the direction of your hopes and dreams? What makes you think that you're not good enough? Please don't tell me it was something that someone said to you, years and years ago. Or, maybe it was just yesterday. No matter when you chose to adopt the attitude of fear, which automatically attracts low self-esteem and lack of confidence in everything that you do, you are allowing yourself to be victimized by your own self-generated thoughts of failure and defeat. You see, the reality is that whoever initially made some stupid or degrading remarks to you in life has been given too much power and control over you and they may not even be aware of this impact. So, if you are allowing yourself to be subjected to this kind of torment, you're actually keeping the fear alive. Why in the world would any woman want to do this to herself?

It's about time us girls united as one in the concept of accepting each other as God's gift to this earth. As women, we are nurturers and healers. We have the capability to create life within our bodies. Why do we often attack one another when God our creator blessed us with so much power? For those of us who are mothers, we should be nurturing to each other. Stop tearing your sisters down and build each other up as acts of kindness. Life is created within a woman's womb. From here, love is established upon the earth. Therefore it's time to let go of all the wrongs that have been done to you. The internal pain that you are carrying inside is slowly destroying the essence of who you are. This kind of decay will deteriorate your spirit and emotions on so many levels. If allowed to continue on this negative path, it will eventually affect your physical and mental health. Again, how SEXY is that?

Reflecting on my childhood years, I recall attending Sunday school classes where I was taught about forgiveness. Don't ask me the details, but this I can say: forgiveness has been a HUGE part of my life growing up. I can't even count the amount of times people have let me down, tried to destroy my faith, hope and dreams. Yet, I always forgave them. I was brought up in a home where strong moral values were instilled and even enforced and I have come to learn there is so much more to forgiveness than telling someone you forgive them. For instance, I have had to literally switch my mindset from that of being victimized to the understanding that whomever it was that had offended or hurt me was actually the one to be sorry for. You see, as I have come to my own understanding, broken people create more broken people. People who have been damaged to some degree are more likely to hurt others subconsciously or otherwise, unless they have sought counsel or advice about their actions and behaviours. Choosing to forgive is a very powerful act of releasing your offenders. You don't need to be in the same room as them, and you don't even need to talk with them. However, if you do interact often, it would be wise to tell them you have forgiven them. It could be in writing or over the phone. The bottom line is that you are more than good enough.

It has not been an easy journey to get where I am in my life now. I have personally walked through so many forms of rejection and hate by people in my life. But, I have to be honest, even without the training and research that I have accumulated throughout the years, the naïve and uneducated little girl I once was still had the willpower and confidence to believe in myself when others did not. I am proud to say that somewhere in the midst of my uncertainty and low self-esteem as a young immigrant girl from Guyana, South America, I still managed to find the strength to let myself believe that there was so much more to my life than the negativity I faced growing up in a small Northern-Ontario community. You see, I decided that I had something big to accomplish in my life and just as I am saying this to you now, I also believe that you too have something big to accomplish in your life. I have come to understand that this life is a mystery that is NOT a mystery. As strange as this may seem to you, what I'm really saying is that life is how you choose to make it. It's all about how you choose to accept it and definitely all about what you want to do with it. Each and every amazing and profound experience we walk through was actually meant to happen the way it did, or it would NOT have happened at all.

My personal theory is that there are no coincidences in this life. In fact, I truly believe we allow people to treat us a certain way, until we decide that we don't want it that way any longer. So, then we make changes to shift the flow of reactions towards us. If we are satisfied we change nothing. As a young girl, this was a concept that I did not fully comprehend yet I was aware that I did not want people to treat me negatively or differently. I grew up in a place where I felt that I was being constantly watched because I was different and that being so, I was fully aware that people talked about me. For any young woman, this alone is traumatic and will most likely affect your self-esteem and confidence in many ways. Small communities are notorious for the labels and attitudes that they encourage its citizens to participate in.

The amazing thing I now realize, as an adult who has successfully accomplished all that I have to this point in my life, is that I am actually grateful for all the experiences I have had. It does not bother me any longer how my peers behaved towards me or may have discounted me as a person of value. Because of their attitudes and behaviours, I was able to be my authentic self and discover who I really was at such a young age. My parents were strict and I am thankful for that even though I was rebellious in my own ways. I always had that moral grounding to appreciate that they wanted something better for me and set higher standards that at times felt like living hell as a young adult. Looking back, I have covered all those years with nothing but love. I hold no hard feelings against anyone from my past and trust me, there were some vicious people in my life who know who they are and all I can say is I honestly feel sorry for them. No one should ever treat another human being with so much hate and contempt like they had done towards me for no reason. They just decided to become hateful.

Anyone who can plot despair and demise against another person is someone who is hurting very much. Imagine how messed up they really are? How can they ever be at peace with themselves if they've never made things right with anyone they've hurt? I went through a period in my life where I literally had no sleep for months and lived in turmoil trying to understand why I was being treated the way I was with no explanation or reason.

I was humiliated and degraded. I was challenged and pushed to my limits. That was horrible and I would never want anyone to experience what I walked through. I was on the verge of committing suicide because of the mental and verbal abuse.

Yet, in the midst of my despair, I had this constant reminder from my beautiful mom: God had a plan for my life that was slowly starting to sink in and take root. I realized there was something valuable about me and it must be why I was going through turmoil. I made a decision in midst of my pain to make a window and climb out of my darkness. With that small step of faith, when so much was against me, I managed to find the door to my success.

I have a dream to live for and so do you. Search your heart once more and open the windows to let the light of hope into your world. You will see the door to your success is waiting for you to open as well. God has a plan for your life too. DON'T give up!

Absolutely You Keys for Empowerment #2
*Live without regrets by choosing to be
the best possible person
you can be each and everyday!
You can be a better person today.
You are more than good enough.*

3 I Am a SEXY Genius!

When was the last time that you made this statement: "I am a Sexy and Sophisticated Genius!" Many of us women would be so much more confident in ourselves if we embraced this fact. Isn't it about time that you also realized it and owned that special and inspirational part of who you are. If you keep downplaying your abilities, you will give off the wrong impression of who you are to everyone around you. Why would you want to do that? There isn't anything SEXY about being something you're not. This false pretence that you are showing others creates a façade of who you really are. Your life is then being built on an unstable foundation of wrong perceptions and ridiculous expectations from people who have no idea who they are really dealing with.

So, if those expectations really prove you wrong, why do you blame others for their disappointment in something false? It's about time that you start believing more in yourself and grow independently successful in your own self-esteem and confidence. Once you figure out who you are and embrace your weaknesses, then you can finally start to strengthen every facet of your ingenious persona.

From the moment you were conceived and your passage to this earth started, your cellular DNA began its most magical creation ever. You were lovingly knitted together in your mother's womb: cells, tissues, organs and physiological systems that communicated to each other to release the right hormones and trigger the responses that only you can give to produce the most beautiful and intellectual you. Yes, you are an intricate, complicated and beautiful life form. You are one of a kind. There is no one else like you in all of creation, given your unique cellular make-up and all its complexities. Every experience that you have walked through to this point has brought you to where you are today. So if you have not been living truthfully to embrace and accept how special you really are, no one else can do it for you.

Yet here you are feeling like you are not "Smart" enough. By purposely neglecting the genius within, you are denying your very potential for success in life. Only you can make your own choices in life. You eat, sleep, walk, talk and breathe on your own. Every new day that we are blessed with, we are faced with a myriad of decisions to make, and in the big picture of things, we still accomplish this rather successfully. Reflecting on our earliest of memories, we can begin to see how our inner geniuses have carried us through so many life experiences to where we are now. Yes I can personally say that not every moment of our lives can be glamorous and sexy, but it's still our lives. We are the only ones who can make the best of it. We all have choices to make that will determine our future.

Although we cannot change the past, we can certainly learn and grow from it. Look at how amazing and intelligent you really are. The life that you are living is your own reality and everything you are experiencing on a daily basis responds accordingly. One might even say that your body is a universe within itself and everything that affects you is part of the effects of your own complex universe. How radical is that? Can you imagine?

You can allude to others about your dreams, successes and accomplishments. But you can't change your reality if you can't change your direction. You can embellish the facts about yourself and ignore all you desire to be, but it will not make you any happier. Look inside your heart. Face the facts; learn to accept your failures and disappointments as they happen. You are only human. This is also another way that we grow and develop into the people we want to be, by our choices. If you choose to let it all go, then you can have an open mind to the possibility of the life you often dream of!

Since we've established that you are in control of your life, have you ever considered the power of your thoughts? You see, our mental faculties and foundational mindsets are ironically the power source of what actually enables our lives to unfold the way they do. We fuel our future by the things we generate within our dreams, goals, training, life experiences and progressive theories. So why not start thinking and speaking more "Positive" and "Empowering" statements? Did you know that your words can create or destroy your happiness and success in a split second? As drastic as this may sound, everything starts somewhere. When you look at a large oak tree, you can't see the acorn that rooted deep into the ground to create such a magnificent sight. Yet you can see the result and manifestation of one small seed. Basically what I'm trying to say is that every thought that is reinforced and supported to exist will grow into something that may become larger than life whether or not we realize it. You see, what you feed or fuel by giving attention to encourages it to birth into your reality.

Many times we are not even aware of how powerful our emotions and attitudes really are. Think about things that you have really wanted in your life and then recall when you received them or actually achieved them. These things must have been something you really wanted because you spent so much time daydreaming and being focused on them. Do you realize that you actually tested your "faith" and allowed it to manifest your desires? The thing is, what you continue allowing to be processed through your mind is being put into the production mode of your own world. The Universe does not decipher whether it is a good or bad thing for you. It just gets directed by the energy that you have towards that thought. Just like good things are healing, loving and beneficial for us all, the same is true of our negative thoughts or hurtful words. These will manifest things that are negative and destroy the beauty that wants to shine through you. Such thoughts often become damaging words which are the limitations that you are allowing to prevent your own life from blossoming into everything that you were created for it to become. By staying open-minded, forgiving and releasing negativity and pain, you will begin to ignite your passion buried deep within your soul. It's time to allow yourself to be "You." You are a SEXY genius, and you know exactly what to do.

So now it's time to take control of what you have been allowing to affect your life to such a degree. The obvious is true: we cannot control or change how others react, but we can control or manage our own behaviours and responses. People always show us their true nature one way or another. We must learn to pay attention and not just react carelessly or emotionally. By behaving in a reckless manner we have lowered our own intellectual being. Therefore, strive to be confident in one's self. It is much easier to mange your response to life's unexpected events in the most calm and sensitive way possible. One of the sexiest things a woman can do is to stay in control of her emotional life. It will present you as a calm, confident and intelligent person. By allowing yourself to adapt a state of serenity no matter what you may be facing in life, your integrity will remain intact. By consistently sustaining your composure, clarity will always be your friend.

Remember, your life is yours to manage and control as it is subjected to your behaviours and decisions. It's your personal journey to make powerful choices; sometimes required to be made in an instant. One way to process information mindfully is to "step away" from stressful situations, evaluate the circumstances involved and the possible outcomes. You are the Master of your universe and the creator of your outcome in life based on each of your decisions. Do you remember the last real life lesson you learned? Was it in College or University? Was it last week when you were on the job training? Was it in the parking lot of the grocery store? The very fact that you have the ability to learn such skills and complexities sets you apart from almost every other creature on this earth. You are a sensitive and caring woman. You are capable of embracing all that you are meant to be, if you only believe that you are able!

Can you remember that one thing you have failed at in life? Did it ever stop you from moving forward? I mean, you're still here and you're reading my book. Obviously, those bad grades, poor test scores, rejection and failure did not stop you from walking, talking, eating and reading. You kept living and learning and you continued growing in your creative intellect and abilities.

Many times in my own life, I have questioned my abilities, but have come to understand that if I'm still searching myself for answers, the doubt that I have is an indication that either the situation or circumstances may not be right for me. Through trial and error, I believe everyone has a plethora of past experiences to glean from. We know what our strengths and weaknesses are and we know when we will allow ourselves to be stretched or challenged. So if we're not ready, hesitation usually sets in like a red flag, warning us that the temperature is not right, causing us to step back. I too have struggled with this personal marker in my life and it caused me many times to put myself in a position to step out of my comfort zone because of the goals and dreams that I was determined to achieve in my life. So whatever you may be facing in your life with no results as yet does not mean that you're not good enough, smart enough or right for the part. More than likely, it's just life showing you the potential that is still untapped within yourself.

As creatures of habit with many complexities, we tend to get complacent with our roles and responsibilities. Then one day, which for some can be more frequently than others, based on our individual goals, we finally wake up and determine that it's time to shift our mindsets and incorporate a whole new level of greatness within ourselves.

I encourage you to seek out more opportunities to learn and increase your skill set by continually challenging yourself to become a better version of who you were yesterday.

Considering all the things I myself have experienced, connecting with so many great and not so great personalities, the one thing I can say about my life is that no matter what I have experienced and at times just tolerated, I am grateful that I never allowed my emotional pain or disappointments to redirect my goals in life. Of course, like anyone else, there were times of struggle and moments of despair. Many times it felt like life was so unfair. Yet I pursued my dreams and goals despite the loss and struggles I endured. Not everyone in my life believed in me. You can imagine how that feels like when you would expect your family to be proud of your accomplishments in life. Like anyone else, I have always encouraged and supported my family and I have always loved and accepted them for who they are. You would think that I was reciprocated with the same kind of behaviour. Instead, I had to face a reality of relatives who ignored my achievements and pretended that it never happened. Could you imagine what it's like to listen to them for years boast about their own and totally ignore you? Thankfully I realized at an early age that the gifts I had been blessed with was not everyone's cup of tea, and that was just fine. After all, who had the time to waste over jealousy or spiteful people in life when there's so much more to accomplish and many people are waiting to be encouraged and inspired. I learned that if I allowed their negativity to hurt me any longer, it would burn out my passion and zest for life.

The baggage of jealousy and animosity is too painful to carry. Sadly it is so much healthier and freeing to forgive and release them to their own destructive ways. When people can be harsh to their own family members, how could they ever have a peaceful and happy life? We all have choices to make and are accountable for our actions and behaviours. Don't allow yourself to be degraded and feel like you have no value to contribute to this world. Trust me when I say this: Your gift is so valuable. Be careful who you trust. You are so much better than you give yourself credit for. Let go of disempowering thoughts and everything that is associated with it. Love yourself more and love others for who they are. You don't need to waste your time on someone else's issues. We all have a journey in life. Make yours a smooth ride.

You are smart enough and you are a SEXY genius!

Absolutely You Keys for Empowerment #3

Live in satisfaction for the life you have been blessed with.
You have been given a special gift.
Only you can be the person you were born to be.
You are a SEXY genius.

4 I Am Beautiful and Sexy!

Yes, you are more than beautiful and sexy! It's about time someone told you like it is. How can you continue believing the negative opinions of others; especially those who have no authority to give it unless you allow them to? Why do you think you should lower your self-worth and value to please everyone else around you? Was it something that happened, causing you to believe the lies and painful words just because of someone else's insecurity? Yes that's right. Women are famous for making other women feel insecure and unappreciated when they themselves may be feeling miserable inside. That's right. The secret's out.

Throughout history, women have always used their physical attributes in one way or another to get what they want in life. Don't get me wrong. Not every woman would stoop to this level but due to evolution and its processes, our ancestors often believed that beauty came before brains or anything else. Aside from social status, physical appearance and attractiveness differ among various cultures. But we don't need a history lesson to know and understand that there has always been, and most likely will always be, competition among women.

Our own families are usually where all this animosity begins, whether it is trying to get the attention of either parent or just trying to be accepted by our relatives. I can't even begin to tell you how many times I have heard about the jealousy issues among close relations. Instead of celebrating their loved one's success, aunts, uncles, cousins and even siblings have created so much pain and heartache that families are damaged or even destroyed. What a shameful and sad situation that this type of behaviour is even tolerated and allowed to continue. As a Registered Nurse, I have witnessed so many lives at the end of their journey sadly facing the heartache of estranged family members and the disappointment of leaving this world with unfinished love. Whether it's between loved ones or acquaintances, each life has value and deserves attention. Everyday there are lives that perish for love that is lost and can never be replaced. Bitterness is a poison that tears the soul apart.

Why is it so hard for these people to just be happy and appreciate that they are even related to such an amazing individual? Unless you have a good reason to believe that you are less than the beautiful and sexy woman that you were created to be, why do you keep allowing the opinions of others to ruin your day? After all, you are an intelligent, open minded, and caring person. Are you sure this is how you want to be; insecure with low self-esteem that will most likely affect all your ambitions and dreams in life?

You see, sometimes we believe so much in the people we associate with that it can strongly affect our personal perceptions of how we view ourselves. So if you are having complexities about your appearance, it might be a good idea to ask yourself what kind of influence your friends or family have on you. Are they supportive and encouraging you to see how beautiful you really are? When you care about the happiness and well-being of someone close to you, there are no flaws or imperfections. You can only see possibilities of greatness and unlimited beauty. Your love for that individual becomes important and valuable. You grow to appreciate the relationship and cherish it for eternity. Nothing can change the love that you see within the other person and you will always be supportive and encouraging.

Basically, what I'm trying to say here is everyone is beautiful in their own individual and fabulous way. Beauty comes in all sizes, shapes and colours. So if the people closest to you cannot appreciate and compliment your good looks, beautiful personality and sexy nature, as a woman with greatness inside her, something's not right. It's time to start believing that you are a sexy woman and beauty is your natural trademark. One person's opinion of you does not mean that the whole world thinks this way. Social Media is an imaginary world where so many examples of acceptable beauty can influence anyone about role models who may not even be authentic. Why compare yourself to someone or something else? Isn't it about time to start believing more in yourself than the opinions of people who don't give a damn about your happiness?

Life is beautiful. The very fact that you are here proves that you are a thing of beauty. You have been blessed with an opportunity to appreciate all that you are and all that you can become. If you're not happy with your looks, you can still do something about it. Try changing your hair colour or style. If your current hair dresser has not encouraged you to experiment and try new looks, start looking for a new one. Ask your friends, who have great cuts and styles for recommendations. If you want longer locks, you can even purchase hair extensions on-line. As a modern woman, everything is accessible to you if you desire a new look or even a complete makeover. If you're not happy with your weight, work out and change your diet to a healthier one.

Go ahead, don't be shy. Try out some different fashion styles. There's always a way to make yourself happy. Replace the negativity in your life with more positivity. Start embracing every day with a new attitude of love. Choose to love your life more. Choose to love the little things in your life and then you will be more grateful for the bigger things that will come your way. The greatest thing you can do for yourself is just love who you are. No matter what you do to change your outward appearance, if you can't accept and love yourself for who you are, you won't ever be happy. But if you adopt an attitude of love, you will begin to attract more love and acceptance into your world. Start giving compliments more and become more of a blessing to those around you. You don't have to a sunbeam everyday, but you can start looking at the sunny side of life.

Do you see how beautiful you are now? Have you ever tried volunteering in the community or helping out with fundraising events? Do you have a relationship that has become complacent in your life? When was the last time you evaluated the situation closely. For example: Have you ever gone out of your way to make the other person know that you honestly care for them? If you have already been doing this and still not feel it being reciprocated, or you feel underappreciated, maybe its time consider your options.

First, start with yourself and ask how much you really love yourself. If you love yourself, you would want to be happy no matter what kind of relationship it is: friendship, family or marriage. Put yourself in a place of happiness, beauty and love. Are you doing everything you can to make yourself happy enough? Meaning, are you actually participating and enjoying hobbies or activities that bring out the best in you. For beauty, are you giving yourself a beautiful life? It's time you allow yourself the simple pleasures that can make a world of difference in your perspectives. When was the last time you bought yourself a special gift such as an aromatherapy candle, scented bubble bath, flowers, new make-up, a massage, new gym membership or a manicure and pedicure? There's a difference between shopping to fill a need in one's life and gifting yourself with something that makes you feel beautiful and sexy. It took me years to understand this as I grew to appreciate who I was. I realized that material things could never give me the satisfaction or the acceptance that I was looking for. By understanding the reason I pursued the things I did in life, I saw my value as an individual and realized how much it was needed in this world. As a nurse, I've been able to listen to my patients and understand what they are going through. I may not completely relate to their situations, but by being empathetic I myself was sensitive to their needs. I have provided treatments and care to literally hundreds of people whom I never knew before they were my patients. These experiences have affected my perspectives about life and all that it encompasses.

When you see life begin and witness it end, it will affect you and things that were once bothersome or unimportant can become so much more valuable. You stop taking things for granted and appreciate all that you have been blessed with. It's then that you finally understand the importance of celebrating all that life brings your way. Every milestone that you pass is a testimony to the fact that you are a beautiful creation and this world is a better place because of you. As a woman, you have ample opportunity to embrace your sexy nature. As the days go by we grow older day by day, consider seizing your moments of sexiness today and set tomorrow on fire.

Absolutely You Keys for Empowerment #4

Live in celebration of your womanhood.
You are a beautiful and sexy woman.
Wear the things that enhance your feminine nature
and stop being just one of the guys.
Sometimes a woman needs her own identity.
Your value in the eyes of your peers will increase
because your attitude towards others is sincere.
You are a beautiful and sexy woman.

5 I Really Can Do It!

It's about time that you start believing that nothing is impossible because you believe in yourself. Look how far you've already come in life. When it was easy to give up, you never did.

You are intelligent, beautiful, sensitive and loving. You have everything it takes to get you where you want to go in life. As you create your own thoughts of success, you will start attracting the things you need to get you there. Doors that were once closed will become open and people who are meant to assist you with your life goals will come along side you. Stay positive. Stay focused. Because you are such a kind and loving soul, everything that you touch will be blessed. As you build others up, you are sowing success into your world. Believe in the endless possibilities of what seems impossible now.

Do you recall the things that were once challenging at one point in your life, only to become second nature now? Think back to your baby steps. Can you honestly remember how many times you stumbled and fell? Of course not and now you can even walk in all kinds of high heels! After all, you are a sexy genius and beautiful to boot.

Your creative intellect has already witnessed the success of your dreams right on your pillow. If you can dream it, you can achieve it. Don't give up so easily on yourself. Too many women are already doing that, believe it or not. Your dreams and ambitions were given to only you from the heavenly realms and have existed before time.

Our thoughts create our reality as we know it. But we still need to positively and enthusiastically speak it into our lives. As we pray, meditate and acknowledge how strong and courageous we really are, we can start to believe more in ourselves. You see, you are a woman of integrity and full of love. As you encourage and motivate others, your passion for success continually grows within you. There isn't anything that's too difficult if you really believe in the reason behind your goals. Sometimes labels are placed on us throughout our lives and it becomes like a piece of garment that we continue wearing even though it feels uncomfortable because we know that we have outgrown it. However, for the sake of not causing distension among our peers, we choose to be uncomfortable, restricted from reaching out towards our goals and ambitions in life. This is how many dreams have sadly perished or have been aborted before they even had a chance to live.

Why do so many women often choose to believe the lies, labels and limitations placed on them from others when they could so easily toss it out? From my own experience and through the experiences of my friends, family, colleagues and clients, I have come to understand that we all just want to fit in and be accepted. It is far easier to shut up and put up with the crap from our so-called support system than speak up and create the "dreaded drama" which may put us at risk for losing these relationships. There is nothing more discouraging than associating ourselves with dream killers and destiny destroyers, we all have at some point in our lives been around or associated with people who are quick to discourage and cause us to feel less than important. You see, jealousy has no boundaries. In fact it is one of the most painful realities of being human; our competitive nature to progress in life can easily overtake even the best of intentions if we don't keep our level of satisfaction about life in check.

The truth is there's no room for limitations in your life if you really want to believe more in yourself. Only you can determine what is fair and what is false, your intuition can tell you so much based on your own experiences and that which you have learned from. I encourage you to start believing more in yourself and let go of all the lies and ugly words that have spoken about you. Do you really want to waste another day stressing about things that have nothing to do with you, but ultimately point to the people who really have issues with their own reality and insecurities around you? The more that you educate yourself and develop the skills necessary to accomplish your goals in life, the more successful you will be. It really is that simple. In fact, it's only as difficult as you make it to be.

Everything worth achieving in life begins somewhere. Even the teacher was once a pupil. As women, we have special roles in this world. Women are natural born leaders because we become mothers who nurture and train the future generations.

We can conceive life and carry it for nine months as it is developing beautifully and perfectly within our wombs. That little baby that you give birth to grows day by day to become a handsome and strong young man or a beautiful and courageous young woman. Can you now see how beautifully life unfolds around you? It's time to stop letting your limitations get the best of you. You were born to succeed and you were a success the day that you took your first breath. It's about time for you to be happy in every area of your life. If you're not completely satisfied, what are you going to do about it? Like I mentioned before, only you can make a change. No one else can do it for you. It's your life and you're in control.

We cannot change anyone else but ourselves. Everyone and everything responds to our actions and behaviours.

Choose to only make positive and motivating statements about your life and all that makes you the amazing and beautiful woman that you really are. Your opinion of yourself is all that should matter when it comes to you. If there is something you really want to do in your life, start asking yourself what you need to accomplish this. Daydream a little longer, but make sure that you allow yourself to become emotionally connected to your dreams. Taste them, touch them and discover what they feel like. Try them on for size to see if they fit. You can often tell if the dream is worth pursuing by the challenge. If it's too easy, then it's not really your passionate dream that will keep you going and get your wheels turning. Often we can get side-tracked easily by temporary goals and ambitions that may seem like they belong in our lives but they are actually stumbling blocks. Even though our actions may get us moving along in life, they will not get us very far if they are not fuelled by passion with a purpose. If our daily goals are holding us back longer from moving forward successfully in the direction of our big life goals, then it's time to re-evaluate our actions and understand why we keep putting off what would actually make us happy and feel accomplished in life. If your smiles shine brighter and your passions push you to climb higher, you know you don't have to try so hard any longer. You will know and feel the difference because you have the excitement and endurance of a bright and shining star!

Life is a gift and many times I even question why I am not doing everything that I know I should be doing right now. It has taken me many trials and errors along my journey to finally do things that I know I can do. What I've discovered about myself is that once I finally accept my ambitions, it becomes so much easier to accomplish things. I admit that many times, there have been goals that were achieved with no prior experience, just sheer determination to do something new and prove to myself that I'm capable and more than able to do what I set my heart to do. At first it can be quite intimidating and just like everyone else, I've had moments of making excuses and looking for reasons why I should not do something I really wanted to. But then I came to my senses quite quickly after realizing I'm the only one who can motivate myself to get moving in the direction of my dreams. I discovered if I allowed myself to feel the fear of the unknown, I'd stop moving. But once I told myself I could do this, I quickly recovered my game. Any fear or hesitation that I may have allowed myself to focus on immediately dissipates and completely disappears into the past. Based on my own experiences, I strongly believe that anyone who has the courage to hold on to their ship while going through the storms of life, such as stretching to fit into new roles and responsibilities, is one of the best ways to prove to yourself that you are a person of integrity and the captain of your ship who can walk their talk. This is what leadership is all about.

One of the most satisfying things in life, if you are a goal setter, is accomplishing the things that you once looked at as difficult tasks to conquer. How's that for being ambitious? This is one of the easiest ways to build your confidence and self-esteem in life and know how special and pretty powerful you really are. All the things that people may have once said to you or spoken about you can be proven wrong. You are a fantastic person and anything that you set your mind to can be accomplished. You can do it and with a little faith, you can go farther than you once thought possible!

Absolutely You Keys for Empowerment #5
*Live freely in the moment, by enjoying
each and every opportunity that permits you to be
exactly how you want to be. You have freedom to be you.
You really can do it!*

6 I Was Born to STAND Out!

Of course you were born to stand out! There's no one else like you. You are one of a kind, original and true. Why in the world would you ever want to just fit in when every team needs a leader? Every ship needs a captain and every path in life needs someone to step out and show the way. Not everyone is comfortable being stretched out of their comfort zone, but if your desire to make a difference is stronger than being comfortable, you have big shoes to fill.

As a born leader, you have greatness within you waiting to be released into this world. Perhaps you came from a family of successful entrepreneurs, or maybe you were the first in your family to step up. Whatever your heritage is doesn't define who you are. Your journey in life is unique to you and your compass is the passion growing within your heart. No matter what you've walked through already, every path that you have crossed has brought you to exactly where you need to be. Don't doubt the powers that be. There are no coincidences in life and every choice that you have made in poor judgement or with careful consideration has all been re-routed to pave the way for your destiny.

As a woman you should never let it become a burden or discouragement if you have to work harder to prove yourself. Sometimes we can easily deny the victory of our success because we are so distracted by who's playing the game and who's cheating. So What! Just keep going. You don't have to give up on yourself so quickly. Don't stop now as the best experiences are yet to come. Allow life's adventures to unfold before you. Often times we don't appreciate the struggles or trials we endured and easily forget the things we learned about ourselves along the way. It's time to stop looking for your confidence in others. You can keep building others up and supporting their dreams and visions, but when are you going to wake up and realize that no one is supporting yours? It's true that not everyone is cut out to be a leader just as not everyone can continue being a follower. Although many are content with these roles, there is nothing wrong with challenging yourself to step into your big picture reality. Have you looked at yourself in the mirror lately? Do you like what you are seeing? If you're not satisfied with the picture that you have painted so far, go ahead and make the changes that are needed to get you where you want to go. Stop waiting for permission from others and take ownership of your life.

So far we've covered self-image, self-confidence, intelligence and self-esteem. For sure you must know by now where you stand in originality. As an authentic leader, you've always been drawn to standing out in the crowd whether you actually did or not. When you have a calling for greatness in your life, you will be miserable if you don't step up to your role. This is your true nature. You don't need a crowd of followers. You already know deep within your spirit that you have something of priceless value to share with the world. Don't let yourself be silenced by your fears of failure or inadequacy any longer. These insecurities you carry inside must be put in their place once and for all. You don't need negative energy to distract you from success in life. Remember, what you focus on becomes a reality so it's time that you change your disempowering thoughts to ones of success and triumph! I know you can do this, and so do you. Just like you've already supported and encouraged others in the past, it's time for you to finally step up and believe the same for yourself.

There's no greater moment in a leader's life than when they realized how significant they really are. Leaders must choose to love themselves first so that the inspiration they carry within will survive the test of time. You have always given unconditional love to others through your passions and dreams. By doing so, you are creating a legacy of the leader that you already are. People want someone who is genuine and confident for what they believe in. I don't know what kind of leader you see yourself as. Maybe you're a volunteer in an organization that helps underprivileged families. Your leadership skills and ideas will help so many innocent lives and future generations. Don't give up on yourself. Maybe you want to start an employee support group for single mothers. Your guidance will inspire other women to see hope where they thought there wasn't any. Maybe you have a great initiative how to raise funds for orphanages in Africa or other third world countries. Go ahead and develop your plans. Write them out and develop your proposal. Then seek out a support system. Don't give up! There's a whole world waiting for you to step out and into your role as a visionary of hope. The more that you love the life that you have been blessed with, the more you can bless others to live.

A leader does not always have a certain look or fit a specific description. Instead, they tread through much opposition or criticism. It's not an easy job when you are breaking new ground. You will face hardships and struggle with your confidence, but if you remain strong in your opinions and points of view you will have maintained a solid foundation to stand on. This is the platform that you need to bring others onto.

Every leader needs faithful followers along side and it starts with believing in one's self. It's time to be real and accept who you are when you can no longer sit by and watch others accomplish things that they once only talked about. You know that you have the requirements to contribute to the greater good. Start loving your dreams and ignite them with the motivation needed to keep moving confidently in this direction. Part of this self-love requires letting go of everything that has ever hurt or discouraged you from feeling loved and perfect in your own special way. You don't live in the past and it's time to let go of all the memories that have suffocated your strong and sexy nature from stepping into what you were born to be.

As I reflect on the things I have already lived through, I can see where I struggled with my self-view and at times strongly disliked who I was more than I cared to acknowledge. I was not the smartest in my classes growing up nor was I the prettiest girl (but I was still cute) I was the last kid picked for teams in gym class and not always invited to all of my classmates' parties. I had my own little group of friends and like any teen I had to find my voice and identity in this world. But I had dreams and with those dreams I was able to build a life of success by believing more and more in myself. Now as an adult, I can say that I have faced head on the academic limitations that once hung over me. I successfully completed my Nursing Program with the highest grades in my first year and graduated with excellent standing as a Registered Nurse. Never in a million years did I think I could learn to love math. Because I was faced with a decision that determined my future, I chose right there and then to shift my mindset and attitude about one of my most challenging subjects in school. By embracing this course with an open mind and positive attitude, I successfully achieved the highest grade required. From this experience alone, I can honestly say that if my former instructors could not see the potential within me, then it was my responsibility to see it within myself.

Because I am a positive person and deep thinker who likes to laugh and have fun, I always have a loving and passionate personality about life and the different experiences it brings to me. My faith has always kept me grounded. I value my own beliefs as it has carried me through many hard times in the past, but I would never allow religion to affect my opinion of others. I enjoy having the qualities of a motivator, dreamer, writer, and researcher. I believe that every life has a passion or something of unknown value that is buried deep inside, just waiting to be brought out and released to its greatest potential. My question to you is what does it take to bring your passion or dreams to life?

I love to see lives transformed for the better. In my professional careers, I've seen what happens when life's passions are left untouched and dreams lost forever. I've learned how valuable time becomes when we've made an internal choice for change. Your new positive perspective will get you further ahead than you can imagine. In my personal life experience, I've learned having a positive perspective will keep you stronger and more focused. I've learned it is better to not let your dreams fall to the ground no matter what others' opinions of you are. All that really matters is if you think you are worth it. There's a reason you've been given a dream when it could have landed on anyone else's pillow. You too have come a far way in life and you know the things that once discouraged you. Isn't it time you stopped letting your value be determined by people who have nothing to do with your best interest? Go ahead and give yourself a chance to stand out. Be loud and be proud. Be positive and passionate. You have all it takes and it's time to take your stand. You are a born leader!

Absolutely You Keys for Empowerment #6
Live to be a blessing to others.
You can be kind and show acts of love and appreciation for everyone around you. Someone needs your kindness to help them along in life.
Everything you do is a gift to those around you.
You were born to STAND out.

7 I am Just What They Want!

Just because you've been rejected at various times in your life does not mean you are defeated. In fact everyone gets rejected or discouraged at some point in their lives. This is the way life teaches us to love and appreciate all that it has to offer. It's also another way to determine that it may not have been the right time for what we thought was meant for us. In many ways what we refer to as rejection may actually be a blessing that helps us to re-evaluate our situations and discover if there is anything better that we can do differently the next time. Our perceptions are the key and we get to choose how we will allow life events to unlock and reveal our destiny. By flipping the negative into a positive, we are making what may have been a horrible experience become a catalyst that propels us forward powerfully into our goals and ambitions.

I believe that if we were to develop a habit of always researching and analyzing our choices in life first, we would find the clarity and understanding we are questioning within and in doing so discover how to continue confidently in these decisions with no regrets.

However, I still like to think that when we are caught up in a less favoured direction, we are still travelling towards our goals as long as we don't give up on them so easily. Adapting an attitude like "I am powerful with unlimited potential ready to be unleashed from within me" helps us to attract exactly what we are looking for in life. Our magnificent universe will always give us what we want because what we desire in life also wants us too. Like attracts like. Aren't you glad that God our creator made it so achievable for us to get all the desires of our hearts? Yes, it's true. It may not be easy at first to open yourself to this concept, but as you continue replacing negative thoughts and outcomes in your mind with positive pictures and emotions, you will begin to see the shift happening in your own world.

I have discovered through my own personal experiences that sometimes what I want in life may be easier to achieve than I realize. This usually occurs after I have already made it so complicated. You see, when we have struggled for so long to get things right but yet keep messing it up, we begin to doubt ourselves what our true purpose is in life. This kind of complacency is common among many people. Don't be so hard on yourself if you have to put things in specific order or categorize it before you can fully comprehend your plans. Sometimes if we just give ourselves a chance, we can learn to wrap our minds around it logically. Then the process to follow the execution of our plans becomes comfortable. So if something does not make rational sense and we can't adapt our intellect to understand it, we may have roadblocks to success before it has even been established.

All this complexity either increases our curiosity to understand the unreasonable perception behind it or it discourages our faith in everything surrounding the task at hand, as we tend to toss it out altogether. Our life experiences have shown us that if it can't be proven with solid facts, there is no point to it. So what I'm trying to say is that if we were to examine life through the Law of Attraction perspective, we would discover how our experiences can be so much more positive and productive if we would only choose to look at it that way. This fantastic shift in our mindset will empower our relationships, career goals, financial goals and especially day-to-day life. But like everything else we have to learn to embrace our emotional intelligence more often and understand that our every thought helps to create our realities. If you were to always look at life this way there would be no reason to get so bent out of shape. Instead, we can simply focus on happy and satisfactory outcomes and send out the right kind of positive energy vibrations into the universe which will boomerang back what we put out there. Now can you imagine how powerful your thoughts and emotional responses can be?

If we can begin to switch our mindsets to believing that "I am consistently opening doors of success into my world", then we will actually start seeing those doors of opportunity opening for us. We are using our master key to the universe of unlimited possibilities. You see when we change our frame of mind to help gain a positive attitude towards our past failures; it now becomes a productive life experience and lesson. We can totally start to appreciate all that life has brought to our front door in order to prepare us for the best.

As a world changer, our minds must constantly encourage positive reinforcement through our confident attitude about ourselves. Such as "I am confident that the right doors are opening up to welcome and inspire me more as I choose to be grateful for all that life has already blessed me with. There is so much opportunity for me to continue becoming all that I was created to be. I am a strong leader and all leaders encounter some set-backs in life. I will continue focusing on all that is positive and powerful! I will always believe for a better outcome in everything that I set out to accomplish."

Sadly, many people especially women do not realize that FEAR is a dream killer, if you continue allowing it to be accepted into your world then you most likely will start to believe there is nothing more for you in life. By this time, if fear has succeeded, it will suck the best out of you. Because you are the only one who understands yourself, you have the solution to the perceived problems that may arise. For example, if there is something about yourself that is not helping you to be accepted by your peers and colleagues then you must decide what you can do about it. More than likely, it may be just a matter of nerves.

Not everyone is a social butterfly, so it's perfectly alright to give yourself a chance to start admiring your own qualities. The more that you appreciate who you are will outwardly enhance your personality and social skills. If you tend to stay away from social activities and functions in your community, you will more than likely feel intimidated and insecure around people whom you rarely associate with. The fastest way to decrease these insecurities is to fill your social calendar and get your "heebie-jeebies" blown away. Don't adapt a victim mentality. Remember, it's your life and anything can change if you want it to.

Far too many good people have been controlled and discouraged by this kind of negative draining energy. Why is it that something this damaging can be so easily accepted by people who are intelligent and have so much potential inside of them? I love to encourage everyone to focus on the positive side of things. Although not everything may turn out exactly how you want, with the right attitude you can make great things happen for yourself just like that.

Sometimes it only takes a moment to reflect on the disempowering emotions generated by fear. Unfortunately far too many women allow themselves to be intimidated and back away from their heart's desires because they have allowed themselves to be controlled to the point that the fear of the unknown has become so powerful and overwhelming that they cannot live the life they want.

Believe it or not, doing the following simple exercise below will help you to stay focused. You see, when you closely examine what effects fear can have on your emotional, mental, spiritual and even physical health, it becomes quite obvious why it can be called a dream killer.

That being said, it's perfectly okay to continue dreaming about your success. In fact, dreams are your future set in motion. To take control of your fears, allow yourself to imagine what it feels like to be living it out loud. What kind of details are your dreams made of? How can you own your goals and make it personal to you?

You know exactly what you want. Examine your emotional connection to your goals. If you can taste it, touch it or feel it, you can certainly achieve it. Now take a moment and write down the areas of your life that are significant to you. Example: family, career, finance, health, etc. Now write down what your goals are for each of those areas in six weeks, six months, one year and five years from now. Once you do this little exercise, you have established a blueprint to use as a guide. Whether or not you follow through with it is yours to determine, but I'm pretty sure that once you stop changing your goals you, like most other people, will do everything that's required of you to make it happen.

Nothing is impossible to what you believe in and you're exactly what they're looking for.

Absolutely You Keys for Empowerment #7

Live as an example to those around you.
Make wise decisions in your life, be polite.
Speak kindly of everyone you meet in life.
You don't know how blessed you really are
until you realize that someone needs your help.

8 True Love Will Find Me!

We've all heard it before: love is universal and makes the world go around. It is one of the most talked about subjects in the history of mankind. You and I are created from the unconditional love of our Creator and we are more than capable of giving and receiving love. Because you are the epitome of love, everything you touch will be blessed by this power within you. There isn't anything so powerful and profound in the entire world, yet it still remains a highly sought after mystery and grand prize for all who find it. We must keep in mind that life is not perfect. There will always be some kind of disappointment in a woman's life ranging from one extreme to another, whether its competition, jealousy or lack of confidence, every woman experiences at least some kind of uncertainty in their lives. But it does not mean that it is your fault. If you're still single, it's not the end of the world. Could it be possible that you have not completely found yourself?

Love without borders

When was the last time you allowed yourself to just fall in "LOVE?"
Were you thinking very hard or did it just happen like that?
Did you know before you stepped up to the plate what was next?
What's happening inside you?
Was the feeling intense?
Did you know if it could be real?
What made you stop and take a second look?
Why were you so surprised when things just made sense?

Are you feeling Empowered? Enlightened? Encouraged? Elevated?
Does everything just come naturally?
Was the connection unbelievable or are you still in denial?
Are you still in fear of what's happening deep inside?
Are you trying to reason with yourself?
Are you still putting things into place or changing your perspective?
Was it sudden or did it just develop in a way that you had no control?
Do you still have butterflies?
Will you take it for granted and allow anything to happen?
...or will you nurture it and let it develop into what it is meant to be?
Do you have the patience to stand close and shower it with the love and attention it deserves?
How long are you willing to wait?
Do you understand the intensity behind the words and emotions?
Are you playing games or are you mature enough to handle the explosion of passion that is building up deep inside?
LOVE can make you rich, break down barriers, destroy hate, change lives, reroute destinies, rebuild nations, empower the weak, enlighten, rebuild hope, open deaf ears, and conquer fears.
Love can give vision to the blind and still save your life and all of mankind!
Love can correct the wicked, ignite passions, stop wars, correct mistakes, heal the broken, and save the lost.
Love can connect the pieces, restore the years, and then seal two lives for all eternity!
Love IS the Fountain of Youth!
Are you ready to live a life full of "Love without Borders?"
Always have an open heart to love and accept all as you would want to be loved and accepted.
Trust your heart, feelings, and deepest secrets with only but a few.

Many do not want to change or even understand this significance because they may not have ever been treated with this kind of love, courtesy, and respect.
Do no wrong or harm to others. Why would you want to?
If you have a forgiving and gentle heart, you can be strong enough to let go of what does not make you a loving person.
Why be like something you don't admire, trust, and appreciate?
Live and let live with the knowledge and enlightenment to distinguish the difference between what is real and what is not!

~ Anita Sechesky

As you've read in prior chapters, everyone has a personal challenge they're consciously or subconsciously working on. On a conscious level, we're fully aware of where we screwed up and what we could have done better. So in our minds, we tend to role play the better outcomes with a great ending, not reality but still cathartic in its own special way. On a subconscious level, we have allowed the disappointments and pain to affect us to the core. Because we don't acknowledge it and move on, it becomes part of our daily lives. We eat, sleep and breathe our failures without even realizing it: not healthy and very stagnating to moving forward successfully into any new relationships. Until we can come to a resolution of accepting lost causes and broken hearts as a part of life, it becomes challenging and for some, even debilitating to move past the pain. Time heals but so does the right attitude. Now that you're ready to find the love of your life, you must stop carrying and replaying in your mind the emotional memories of all failed relationships. It's not your responsibility to continue dragging it around, especially if the other person has moved on. Instead, begin the process of loving yourself more each day and a little forgiving wouldn't hurt either. You can start by giving yourself more opportunities to instantly shift your frame of mind. As you incorporate this positive perspective, it's amazing how quickly your passions will come alive within you. Once you realize you don't need to work through the emotions, but just acknowledge and release them for what they are, you'll also release yourself from the emotional ties of these past experiences. By forgiving the other person, you're actually healing yourself and giving your heart room to blossom once again.

Therefore, you must believe that true love will find you when it's the right time, so don't try so hard. Or maybe you've been hiding or sabotaging yourself and not actually realizing it. I would like to encourage you to closely examine the kind of energy that you are carrying around your space. Yes that's right. We all carry our emotional baggage on the outside without awareness. In fact, there are some people so skilled at reading behaviours and body language, they don't even need an introduction. You see, what you may not realize is if you have not addressed rejection or failure in your life from past relationships, then your body language will tell a whole different story than what you are presenting to the world. Maybe it's coming across in the way you dress and present yourself, or in your communication and attitude. The picture you're painting becomes a mish-mash of personality and perceptions, which is conveyed as very confusing and presents a different description than what you're trying to portray.

In order to even have a good relationship with another person, we must love and respect ourselves first. If we cannot find a happy medium in our own lives, how can we ever have time to build a strong foundation with anyone else? We have to be satisfied and content with our lives since we attract and effortlessly shift our world by attracting people who relate to and compliment the internal environment within us.

It's been said many times that being in a relationship will not make you happy if you're unhappy with who you are. What a concept! As repetitive as this might sound to some, please bear with me and let me explain: You see, the reality is we must discover our passions in life sooner rather than later or we may risk never being fully satisfied with the life we have. Your passion will help you uncover your purpose and direction. These two things alone are very powerful and life altering. For men and women alike, it is considered a blessing to find your passion before finding your life partner or soul mate. Through your adventures, you are discovering your authentic self. What better plan than to build yourself up so the right person loves you for exactly who you are. The reason I refer to these perspectives is that one can still find their true love and become successful along the way. Please keep in mind that being in a secure relationship will enhance who we are as it complements your whole life picture.

So, that being said, let's get a little personal and talk about what is really going on with this whole "single wanting desperately to be needed" attitude. For example, is it possible you may be a little too desperate for love without realizing it? There is absolutely nothing wrong with strongly desiring to belong in a loving and supportive relationship. Because we usually tend to attract what we focus on, what is emotionally taking place on the inside at any given time will manifest itself on the outside. So my suggestion for those of you struggling with your love identity: Have you considered finally letting go of what has never worked for you? Everybody has a theme in the way they socially interact to attract a mate. So maybe some of the things you did before didn't play out so well. It may have been fun at one time, but let's face it: games are for children and it's time to get serious. Who wants to keep tossing their heart in the field only to get it trampled on? Aren't you tired of going after the person you want only to be disappointed after becoming so involved with them? How about the way you felt when you couldn't be yourself around them because you were so busy being the faithful and devoted girlfriend? Yet, your partner continued being exactly who they wanted to be around you.

I've often heard my single friends complain that dating is like an Olympic sport. There are so many qualifiers and just when you think you have the gold after enduring so many penalties, and you think you're in the home stretch, reality steps in ... it's just all wrong. Give yourself a break and stop being so hard on yourself. Every relationship requires two committed individuals to play fairly and to be completely satisfied with one another. Honesty is one of the biggest factors. It's not okay to be yourself with just your friends and family and then be somebody different with your partner. Burning the candle at both ends will only get you burned. Authenticity is where true love gets its spark.

One of the interesting things I often hear people coming out of a relationship talk about is regretting all the things they couldn't do during that particular relationship. Why is it there's always so much regret about just living your life? Yes, I understand roles and responsibilities of having a life, but if you're in a trusting relationship with someone who cares about you, then why are you not trusting yourself to be all that you should be? I think that before anyone gets serious, you'd want to know exactly who you are getting involved with. So what I am saying is: All those previous relationships were just stepping stones bringing you to the reality that you'll never truly be happy until you love exactly who you are and all that makes you the beautiful, sophisticated, sexy and intelligent woman that you are.

Now you can start enjoying everything you do in a more magnificent and supercharged way by understanding you are more powerful than you once appreciated. You can easily eliminate negativity, loneliness, fear, rejection and failure out of your past memories. Everything that has been pre-programmed and stored in your "heart files" database should be routinely erased and replaced with an upgrade of new "software." Just like your computer gets bogged down by viruses or old programs that affect its functionality and corrupts its normal processes, so can we get bogged down if we don't maintain the upkeep of our emotional state. This can painlessly be accomplished by focusing on the things that make you happy and bring increased joy and beauty into your life. As you immerse yourself in this renewed way of living, it is easier for love to be attracted to you. You won't even have to try. People are drawn to authenticity, not desperation. Your life will blossom and what you used to dread will become a distant memory. In fact, it will be so much easier to envision yourself in a sweet and loving relationship. If you're having difficulty taking ownership of the life you desire, consider flooding your free time with romantic movies, romance novels, or social outings to meet new people with your friends. Mostly, allow yourself to stay open-minded. Remember, being content with your life is more important than being in a relationship where you're not genuinely satisfied. Every prince desires to find his princess too. And now that you're awake, your beauty is shining through even brighter than before. So don't ever let yourself believe the lies of loneliness any longer. You have your whole life ahead of you waiting to be revealed. With so much going for you, you deserve only the best.

Absolutely You Keys for Empowerment #8

Live confidently knowing that you're perfect in every way possible.
There is no else like you.
Your true love will find you
because there is no one else like you.

9 Marriage is Passionate, Secure and Sexy!

Hello Honeymooners! Are you still feeling the love or do you feel closer to your fuzzy blankets lately? Marriage is supposed to be Passionate, Secure and Sexy! I want to encourage those of you on the partner-ship of marriage to not give up so easily if you feel the flames starting to fizzle out. You know how much this relationship means to you, but it's not all about you. It's about the dreams you share together and the life you make as one. I don't know how long you've been together and it doesn't even matter as long as you haven't thrown in the towel as yet.

Let's be honest and let's get real, girls, for a moment. Life itself is a challenge. But look how amazing you are; choosing to share this journey with another person. It takes a special individual who is selfless, caring and kind to dedicate themselves faithfully in love. Like any relationship, marriage has its own unique complexities. Not everyone is fully prepared to understand what this really means in the beginning of matrimony. After all, life doesn't come with an instruction manual and neither does marriage. Every person is different and brings their own luggage on board. For some, this means childhood memories, dreams, past relationships, family expectations, emotional baggage, and so on. These are just a few of the intricacies that can make the relationship strained if either partner is not ready for so much added responsibility. If you've already been introduced to these issues and realized that it's not just superficial any longer but real life drama, then you are stronger than you understand. As a wife, you're your partner's biggest fan and loyal supporter as your partner should be for you also. Every marriage must have equality and balance to survive the test of time. Throughout this relationship, you will face many obstacles that may or may not be related to the marriage. However, it's the trust and support that will get you through because love is what *will* keep you together. No one knows what the future holds, but keeping the lines of communication open in the busyness of life will save a lot of stress and heartache. If you can always remember who you were when you fell in love, tenderness will never be lost or forgotten. There really is no secret to a happy marriage except remembering that the person you are married to is an individual who just needs to be accepted, loved and appreciated for who they are. Your role is to always remember this just as you remember to love yourself for who you are. As well, love your partner for supporting and encouraging you to be the best version of who you strive to be.

Have you allowed your marriage to become so complacent that there was more excitement when you were first dating? If so, then the red flags are flapping wildly. Something needs to get your attention and this may be the wake up call that you needed. Yes it's true. In marriage we become our partner's best friend but let's face it girls, we don't let our beards grow, get beer bellies, or play rugby with the boys. And if we do, then we have some serious questions to ask ourselves. For instance, all kidding aside, the thing about marriage is that you are supposed to be attracted to the opposite qualities of your partner for sparks to keep flying. If you just allow yourself to become one of the boys then you have seriously disregarded the Sexy and Beautiful woman that you were created to be! What I am saying is that this is not the way a grown up relationship should be treated. How is this even possible after all the stuff we have just covered in the previous chapters? I mean I get it. Marriage can become less than exciting at times because of career, kids and added responsibilities along the way. But the truth of the matter is, I believe many times we allow ourselves to become complacent and if our partner is not doing their part to keep the passion and excitement growing, we immediately point fingers. I can understand that there are times it may be called for and maybe our mate deserves the questions. But if it gets to the point where you are questioning their every move, we have to stop and ask ourselves how did it get so far without noticing the vulnerability of our relationship increasing? Again, please let me remind you ....marriage is supposed to be Passionate, Secure and Sexy! If it is feeling less than that, we have some serious questions to ask ourselves. Remember, we cannot change anyone, including your spouse. So, the best thing to focus on is where we can get back to our reality of why this is happening.

Is there something in our lives that's unfulfilled and is it possible we're not happy with ourselves? The reason I'm bringing it back to us girls is we are a reflection of what's going on inside us and we also magnify wha's going on around us. In a sense we attracted this issue into our lives in some way. Search your heart and determine if you are unhappy. Don't look at anyone else, instead look deep inside your soul and find your love of self once more. Appreciate the things that make you who you are and then inspect to see if you are being all you can be at this very moment. Have you gained weight due to health issues, hormones, or pregnancy? Then don't be so hard on yourself. If you gained weight due to just being unhappy then you must be unhappy with who you are and you need to start realizing how beautiful and sexy you really are. We don't need a partner to validate that we are females and we are perfectly made. Your family and children love you for being yourself. You are the gentle soul who loves and appreciates the things that you have walked through in life. Your journey has been unique to you and you are what makes your marriage so special. Your mate has seen something so precious and valuable in you and chose to spend the rest of their life with you. What an honour! Have you been honest with your mate about who you really are and allowed them to know the real you? As your most loyal and supportive fan, they deserve this and it will actually be beneficial for your relationship. I realize this might seem strange to some but what I'm saying is: Are you being honest with yourself? Maybe you're very careful with your comments about certain things and dislike something they do to the point that it annoys you but you still don't say anything. This is something I could never understand about people in relationships. Often times we think our partner can read our minds! Now imagine what kind of world this would be if that was the case? Great …. not so great! You get the idea; if we want to prevent conflict, allow them to get to know who you are by just being completely honest with your feelings. This way they can work with you to make things compatible and satisfactory for both of you and this means everything! When we can allow ourselves to be vulnerable with our closest relationship we actually strengthen it and develop characteristics that make our connection to our spouse closer and private as it should be.

In doing so we help our mates become vulnerable and open up their own emotions and needs so we build an intimate, loving foundation. As you encourage this communication between yourselves, you'll notice your confidence and self-esteem grow. It will feel like you can do anything and you really can because someone you love, loves you and supports exactly who you are. What an amazing support system you're developing with each other. Many people desire this in their marriage and it's so easy to build, but requires your dedication and faith to believe you deserve this just as much as your spouse. Since they're your life partner, they bring out the best in you. What a blessing! Marriage is almost a novelty these days. When I look around it's sad to recognize how many end in divorce or separation. Often, there are expectations and unresolved personal issues that are brought into the relationship in many form of baggage as listed above but the biggest factor I believe has to do with trust. You see trust is a root that comes from Love. To love someone means you trust them with your life literally and to love them means that your trust is earned. It takes time to get to know someone and love them passionately and unconditionally. Yes, we can love anyone and everyone but marital love is a special kind of love. It's almost considered a selfish love when two people become one, because the only interest and focus is for the survival of the relationship and this is exactly how it should be. Never let it get to the point where your mate is seeking comfort and acceptance elsewhere. This is what home is for, and you're building a love that needs a home and not a ticket to travel. It doesn't matter what you encounter in your journey as a couple. Once you have each other, you can face many situations and come out wiser.

I remember a time in my life as a newlywed when I allowed others to affect my feelings and self-esteem, not realizing that it wasn't about me alone any longer. As first time home-owners, my husband and I loved our house as it was all ours and we took a lot of time and effort to make it the home we wanted. My decor of choice was oak and French Country; the kind of theme that is bold and elaborate with a warm and comfy flair! I was starting to really enjoy decorating especially with my favourite hobby: making all types of dried and silk floral arrangements. My love for flowers had grown tremendously just like our gardens; the more lush the better. Since we had done a lot of renovations after moving in, I took pride in having things a certain way. At this time, our house had just been completed throughout and I had created a HUGE floral decorative centerpiece for my living room. I used the Greek pedestal from our wedding decorations as a vase, so you can imagine how beautiful it was. We had invited another couple over for dinner and as new acquaintances, our families were getting to know each other. What surprised me about this couple was the audacity of the comment made by the husband about my centerpiece saying that it was too "Elaborate!!" I was shocked and didn't know how to respond, so I just let it go. You can imagine my reaction when we later visited their home and guess what the first thing was that greeted me at the door? That's right, a huge "Elaborate" centerpiece. It was almost a complete replica of the one that I had created flowers and all. My husband was even taken aback but still complimented them on the arrangement. Of course I was confused why he did that at the time but when we discussed the awkwardness of the situation later that night, I realized how different it was to face jealousy with someone you care about. This was just one incident, but believe it or not, life has been showing me time and time again the many faces of people. But with a partner, many things that I would have struggled with did not affect me the way it would have if I was single.

When people are quick to judge or find a fault in you it is their own problem because there's something about you that they want, desire or even wish they could be. Some will even want what you have. Start seeing these people for who they are. If they're slowing down your blessings in life, please let them go! As a married woman, you have your best friend and boyfriend all in one. Things once difficult to face alone are now small bumps in the road. As a team, you're so much stronger with two perspectives and one heart. You'll learn to observe that people are trying to get something that's not theirs to begin with or they are just plain jealous. This will save you so much regret later on. I had been the kind of person who allows people to be nasty and take advantage of my kindness. But when you share your life with someone, your dreams become one another's priorities, so you always have someone looking out for you. I've also learned late in life that when people treat you unkindly, ask yourself if they would allow themselves to be treated that way by you. Who needs friends or even family like that? The reality is when trying to step up to a vision that is within your heart, not everyone appreciates it or even understands. But as a wife, you are blessed to have the love of your life support your dreams and ambitions. Over the years I've come to recognize that not many people care to be that way in my own life. A friend loves at all times and she who marries her best friend will always have that love and support.

Because there's so much more responsibility and new roles as a married couple, don't allow yourself to get too comfortable. Keep spontaneity alive and get out of the house once in awhile. Just like when you first started dated....keep having date nights regularly. This way you are giving yourself a chance to stay Sexy and be Sexy! You know exactly what to do to get your relationship hot and spicy and you're allowed to! You only have one life so you might as well enjoy it with your best friend. It's time to bring back what you let go and get back what you let slow down. No one is perfect and your mate is exactly who you wanted when you began this journey together. Yes, I agree we change over time, but there is still room to make it better than it was last week. Start imaging the good days together more often and capture that emotion. Allow yourself to smile and dress up once in awhile just for your spouse. You can still be the passionate woman you want to be and it's not hard considering how Sexy you already are.

Love can last forever. So should real relationships.

Absolutely You Keys for Empowerment #9

Live in agreement with your partner.
Don't allow petty disagreements to take
the best out of your marriage or relationship.
Every loving couple promotes life and a future
that can be passionate, secure, and sexy.

10 Life's a Fantastic Journey

I'm so blessed by the path in life that I am travelling on. This journey has allowed me to be acquainted with so many incredible, beautiful, and amazing people along the way who are honest and loyal with integrity and value. They are leaders in their own right because they understand themselves by knowing how to put others needs first without losing focus on their own goals in life. These people, whom I'm referring to, have left a powerful impact in my life because they are genuine people who will hold you up, add value to your life by appreciating who you are and support you through your own journey!

What fantastic opportunities I have had to converse, share, mentor, and also be trained by these kinds of people and continue attracting into my life. Although I'm still evolving day by day into what I'm striving to become, I prefer to focus on the characteristics of my true authentic self. I appreciate so many diversities and can clearly see things that were once vague to me. Even though I have forged through some tough situations and let things slide as they served me no real purpose, I have still gained wisdom and knowledge from these experiences. I appreciate that not everyone will line up with my vision and that is absolutely alright with me. After all, I choose not to be associated with anyone whose values and integrity disturbs my inner peace and tranquility.

What kind of things have you kept hanging around because you felt you had no other choice but to painfully or uncomfortably tolerate them? Many people are unsure and that's alright. I've been perplexed many times in my life and I now understand things from a different perspective. Although life is an evolution of growth and self-awareness, I'm satisfied and excited where I am at now and how things will progress as I direct my energy and attention towards it.

Everyone can only be expected to comprehend things that they understand based on their own knowledge and experiences. Yet many times it's a personal understanding and if there are unresolved issues in one's life there will likely always be discrepancies of some sort. When these things happen, I encourage you to step back and re-evaluate the situation in a calm and peaceful manner. Appreciate the other person and in doing so allow them their space and vulnerability that they are bringing forward into the relationship. People may react because of their inward man's perception and how it's interpreting the situation around them. When I've been a mediator in various situations, this is the approach I use as people already have many emotions exposed and become vulnerable. I always try to come up with a new perspective and enlightenment. By recognizing the triggers of negativity and harm, we can learn from our previous experiences and grow. Not everyone is meant to be in our inner circle when we are about to reach a new level in life and conflicts can arise at any given time. Communication skills are the greatest asset you can always carry with you.

Our lives are meant to be in a continual state of learning, evolving, and growing into a better and more refined version of who we are than when we started out on our journey to success. Not everyone around us is in that place and many are comfortable right where they are. This is expected as this is how shifts happen. Life allows doors to be closed and new doors are opened to bigger and better opportunities of growth and wisdom that we have been constantly attracting through our thoughts, words, and actions.

In our life we meet so many amazing and beautiful characteristics in the people we connect with. We always attract what comes into our lives by what we are putting out to the universe. Even though some people will inspire and motivate you, many others will still discourage you. But in the big picture it's perfectly alright as it will help you to see things you never noticed previously. I encourage you not to lose hope if someone tries to take advantage of your good nature. Many times you may feel devalued and even unmotivated because you have opened your heart and allowed your vulnerability to be abused. Remember, how someone treats another human being is only a reflection of what is going on inside of them.

There are some people in life who don't care about you, even when you are going through your heartaches and misery. Your life becomes a joke to them.

Yes, it's true. Many times the attitude is: Why talk about me when we can talk about you? Then there are others who don't even want to hear your name. Funny thing about people is no matter what you are going through there will still be those who just don't give a damn. They don't care what you have been through or endured. Their hearts are cold and they just don't want to know. Yes, even if they hear your name, they will shut the door. Don't be fooled thinking because you have some kind of connection, whether it is by association of genetics, education, or career that you are valued by everyone. Some people are just not all that you think they are.

Let your heart not be bruised by their coldness any longer.
Let it all go!
Forgive, Forgive, Forgive!
Be Strong and Carry on!

The best way to always live with peace of mind is to be consistent, genuine, honest, and treat others how you want to be treated. Let go of what does not empower and celebrate who you are. You are better than the bad times you have survived. You don't deserve others trying to bring you down to destroy your dreams and ambitions any longer.

No matter what has transpired, when you start to understand that they do not have the final say over you and your success in life, you will find the courage you need to carry on. Now you can appreciate how to graciously take back the control and power that you need for yourself. This will help you to rise above and see through the smog that you are removing from your life. Only then will things will become clearer and your vision will become brighter.

As we live day-to-day, we are consistently in a self-development mode. Always remember the people who know you as being down to earth and stand by you when they see you in all your dirt will always love you as you are and be there for you. No matter how life changes and breaks you down, it always picks you back up again.

Examine the motives of your heart and let go of all the pain from your past and present experiences. Don't allow yourself to be hurt by it ever again. Don't allow yourself to take all that pain back in!

However, some people will surprise you and want nothing from you except your friendship, smiles, and some of your time.

Let's make the world a better place one person at a time. Remember than many don't have this gift of love inside because it was never given to them in life as yet.

You can make a difference for so many people you meet by making your world a better place. All it takes is being the bigger person. Your smile softens the heart. Your welcomed hug warms the heart. Sometimes it just has to start with you.

Choose to see the ones you can never forget, no matter how life changes and where it takes you. Your real friends are the ones who will love you rich or poor, young or old. These are the ones we all need in our tribe of people we call close by our side to our tender soul in this harsh and lonely world. My heart will always be here with the friends who have been real with me.

I love my tribe! My business tribe is all about enhancing the world in a transformational kind of way. Our greatest resource is LOVE! It's the strongest power in the Universe!

What kind of Tribe are you looking for? Let's be real.

Shine on my dear, sweet friend. YOU are meant for Greatness! Don't let anyone rain on your parade any longer!

I believe in you! Do you?

I am thankful for all the people that I have crossed paths with in my life. I am also grateful for those who are a part of my life right now and into the future. Although not all experiences have been positive at certain times in my life, I now choose if I haven't already done so to forgive and release all the negative garbage. That means ALL the emotionally rooted stuff that I am aware of, or may not even be aware of.

I am grateful for what I have and am expecting an increased overflow of the good things in my life that I strongly desire: a Beautiful and Productive life, a Positive attitude, Happiness, a Healthy mind and body, a Successful marriage, Abundance, and a Blessed family.

I AM expecting excellence in all areas of my life starting right now!

When you choose to be a blessing, then blessings will choose to be part of you.

I was taught at an early age about the Power of Words and Prayer. Forgiveness and love not only make peace in your world, it brings healing to you internally. Life is about choices so choose wisely because everything, every thought, action, reaction, belief, perception, imagination, idealism, lie, truth, knowledge, or wisdom is a factual contribution to who and what we are and eventually become. My feelings about all of this is how "I CHOOSE" to think and live my life.

You will have to decide what works for you and what is not working. Only YOU can make that choice. So choose wisely, because life can only give back to you what you choose to put into it.

Absolutely You Keys for Empowerment #10

Live in good and vibrant health.
We need to start at some point to believe we can be
better physically.
Don't give up so quickly on yourself.
Your body loves you and wants to take of you,
but first you must choose to take care of yourself.
Choose to live your life without limitations.

11 Stay Emotionally Healthy in Your Career

In this chapter I would like to discuss how we can maintain balance and how certain limiting beliefs may influence one's emotional health and well-being. I believe we always need to be enlightened as to what areas are unbalanced and may be distracting, disabling, and even destroying your attempts to maintain a healthy balance in order to achieve successful business ventures.

Our emotional health and well-being can be directly impacted by varying degrees of limitations and become stagnant, ultimately affecting the peaceful reality we so often desire.

Life continues to happen. It is in perpetual motion whether we choose to get out of bed today or not. Things will still carry on as they always do, and because our lives are so connected, we are constantly affected by each other in some way or another. Although we can choose to ignore events or we can filter stuff, we still need to decide how much we will allow things to ultimately affect our lives.

How would you describe your overall emotions today as a modern female business person? Would you say you're a career driven woman who is independent or are you a stay-at-home mom who is starting to make your mark in a chosen field? Either type of business person with high standards and goals would still need some kind of balance to appreciate and thoroughly see the value of their accomplishments in life.

As women, we may encounter many limiting beliefs or ideas when it comes to our professional goals and dreams. These often begin in childhood through labels that are inadvertently placed on us by our families, teachers, peers, and even the stories we read growing up. Many times, without realizing it, we are directed to behave a certain way as society would expect little girls to act, think, and dream. For those of us who choose to break the mould of expectations, our ambitions often defy these labels.

Female entrepreneurs are not immune to the many roles and responsibilities that make them who they are as individuals. If you are a parent, you are nurturing, have ambitions, and provide guidance for your children. You have to be available for them indefinitely with their needs constantly in the back of your mind.

If you're married or have a significant other, you strive to have an open approach to communication, a fun and passionate lifestyle, as well as a stable and trusting relationship. As a child to your adult parents, you make an effort for a peaceful and understanding connection with them. As our parents age, health issues and related concerns require your time and dedication to also be there emotionally. At the end of the day, you still need to schedule time for business training, appointments, social activities, as well as your own health needs such as relaxation, diet and exercising.

I have personally experienced what it feels like to not preserve this stability and then discovered the importance and significance of having it maintained and nurtured so that I can achieve the life I want with a new healthy perspective.

Many women often dream about a life of success that provides security for their families while maintaining control for their own well-being. Even with so much confidence, we may still need appreciation and acknowledgement by those close to us that we have succeeded in our lives. In addition, we need time for personal validation to feel complete; that we've made the right choices. When we have taken control of our emotional well-being, we find more clarity, our creative thought processes begin to flow effortlessly. Things that were once limiting us in our productive capabilities are now removed and replaced by healthy choices.

People who have high standards and are career oriented often face tougher challenges. Many times there seem to be more risks and responsibilities to deal with this way of thinking. We have to be mindful of what's going on in society and how it will impact us. For instance, is the business that we are involved with going to provide a service that is of value and will it be a benefit that's going to give back to others?

When working with colleagues or clients, do we determine boundaries and establish schedules that will empower us by allowing a balance to be created in our lives? Have we organized our social activities? We need to prioritize our time according to the level of importance each area of interest holds.

Our emotional health and well-being is often neglected in many instances because of the responsibilities we carry. There are many solutions to finding stability in all areas of our lives.

Here is a simple two-step exercise that I have successfully used with many of my Coaching clients to help them identify and address areas that are lacking or often neglected:

1) Write down the names of people in your life in order of priority from one to five.
2) Look to see where your name is on the list. Is it there? Where you have placed yourself determines how you see yourself.

Many times people who are high achievers forget to put their name at the top of the list. When this is visually pointed out to them, it becomes a revelation of redefining how they can begin to meet their emotional health and well-being. Without acknowledging where there is lack, a need cannot be met.

The answers to many of our issues lie within our unique emotional perspectives and how we view the world around us. By taking a careful look, discovering where we are at that moment in life, and deciding what needs to be met to find balance, goals can be achieved with no limiting beliefs. Our relationships and businesses will stay balanced and begin to flourish. Once more, you can begin to dream like that little girl with great expectations.

Absolutely You Keys for Empowerment #11

Live in peace and harmony with yourself.
Choose to make the right choices that promote rest and relaxation.
You deserve a stress-free life and it's time to choose wisely!
You can be successful and still stay emotionally healthy in your business and career.

12 Goal Setting is Sexy!

Everyone that desires to be successful still needs to understand how important goal setting is. While maintaining a healthy balance in order to achieve success and enjoy a sexy and satisfying life. It doesn't matter if you're a entrepreneur, student, wife, mother, or even grandmother. Life is demanding and serenity is often fleeting in our personal lives when we neglect to achieve balance on a daily basis. For the purpose of acknowledging career women, I would like to focus on how goal setting is beneficial in their lives although this chapter will help everyone to understand the significance of how it all works together in everything we do.

When starting out in any business you will discover that your personal life will always be affected in one way or another especially if juggling a full-time career and family commitments. Many people, especially female business owners, tend to compromise their activities of daily living with no realistic goals established. What I mean is life moves quickly when you are busy establishing yourselves. Opportunities for happiness are often neglected. Often, responsibilities may feel burdensome and life can become somewhat draining. The benefits of maintaining balance through achievable goal setting results in multiple tasks being accomplished in a timely and successful manner.

Too readily we accept every task that comes to us because of our desire for acknowledgement, achievement, and high standards. This can be recognized by the need to succeed or go forward by moving out of our comfort zones. Since there's only twenty-four hours in a day, we can often neglect of our own dreams and ambitions without realizing it. Most career-driven business women have already moved past the struggle of breaking off limiting beliefs and the mould of average expectations by taking the step forward where others haven't. They have a unique passion and gift that needs to be shared with others and brought to life. Because of this need to birth it into the business world they often find it compromises the focus of their personal goals and requirements for a content and satisfying life.

Also our values as women may affect our decision making and greater risk taking, which can become overwhelming and ultimately make or break our business plans because we fear the loss of friendships and relationships that we already have or even those we want to establish. These pertinent connections which can also be lacking affection and nurturing qualities may leave a person feeling inadequate and believing they don't quite fit in or measure up.

The need to constantly please others often causes many adults to abandon their own goal setting and ambitions. In addition, trying to appease everyone may cause imbalance in business plans, directly affecting our personal lives. With this in mind, many new business owners still have important decisions to make, such as the short and long-term goals needed for their success and longevity.

My question to these women who are still struggling with the need to be accepted and have something unique that they want to bring forward is: How do you find balance between your professional and personal life? When you are concerned about the validation of others, it affects how you perceive yourself and what you can accomplish. If limiting beliefs are holding you back now from being all that you can be as an entrepreneur, how will you get past your fears of failure or success? Have you broken off all the labels from your childhood or has someone told you that you can't amount to anything?

Now is the time to determine where your passion is. This is about you and where you see yourself. If there is something special about you and what you have to offer, your dreams, visions, and goals are what will get you there.

Many times the desire for goal setting can be related to many of our childhood accomplishments. Small steps can bring us further ahead in the big picture. Do you remember how many times you fell off your bike when learning to ride? Did you give up or did you keep trying? The end result is, you did learn to ride your bike independently! Hooray!! Achievable goal setting can be simplified in this way.

Consider this: "Where do you see yourself on a scale of one to five?" Do you find that you're putting yourself low on the list, or are you even there? Have you justified your means by placing yourself at the bottom of the list in order of importance to where you place others? Once you have accepted who you are and the unique qualities that you have to offer as worthy and valuable, you have to believe others will also see this as well.

Goal setting is a common strategy that many Life Coaches use when working with clients. Along with powerful questions asked by the coach, the client determines where they need to be at a certain point in their life. In a professional coaching session, the goals are established with accountability to the coach as a predetermining factor in mind.

Even after goals are agreed upon, life does happen and distracters may cause you from not accomplishing your tasks. I would encourage collaborating with a Life Coach when struggling or feeling stagnant in your perceived dreams and ambitions. People who have taken this route have discovered why they may be emotionally or mentally blocked and not getting further ahead. With an accountability partner which you have given permission to hold you to your own standards, the ability to continue dreaming in living color will become your reality.

We all use goals on a daily basis to get from activity to activity. If we didn't do this, we would never get anywhere. However, when we start branching out as an entrepreneur and bring in added responsibilities, we find establishing clear concise short and long term goals will help accomplish things without becoming overwhelmed and abandoning our plans.

Balancing your business and personal life with goal setting will give you more clarity and freedom to create the life you often dream of. By determining what you feel is achievable in your life according to how you want to live, you automatically start creating a balance between all the important facets that make you who you are as a successful and sexy woman. Happiness can be yours.

Absolutely You Keys for Empowerment #12

Live in expectancy of great and fabulous things!
It's about time that you allow yourself
to believe that you are deserving of all good things.
Let go of the lies and reach for the prize!
Goal setting can be Sexy.

13 Balancing life is an Attitude!

Everyone's life needs to maintain balance in every area to be one that is happy, healthy, and prosperous. Career oriented women are no exception to the struggles and stress that come with the added roles and responsibilities. It's not always easy and sometimes no one understands. However, life is yours to make the best of it and you've never given up before. So let's examine how our attitudes can help us control of the chaos and achieve success in our lives.

What do you think it takes nowadays to become a successful woman? If you are like most entrepreneurs, you have given a fair amount of dedication and sacrifice to put your products or services together. Throughout your journey you have put off doing things that most people take for granted such as pampering yourself or attending special functions. Your dedication has been powerful to get you into action. You have also discovered that you have a unique determination and are willing to give more of yourself towards building your own enterprise.

By now you've realized your schedule should be more flexible than any well known yogi out there. Dedication is the overview, commitment is the glue! Good for you, working a nine-to-five job, going to school, raising your family, or putting your kids through school while building your business. No matter what, with your dreams, you have to be committed to putting in those extra hours. If you don't look past limitations of who you presently are and what you may be going through personally, you can't make a difference and choose where you want to go in your life. In the twenty-first century, business women have become an integral part of a stable economy. Today they're motivated more than ever to get into the work force and make a difference, not only to labour at mediocre jobs but to rise above limiting barriers their own mothers had no choice but to endure. What an example of positive motivation by so many determined and successful women around the globe!

Increasing your value requires you to engage in personal development, training and building skills that demand your valuable, limited time. When everyone's gone to bed you're still up developing your game plan, following through, and working on your marketing strategy. Your success is birthed through these decisions that need your total dedication and commitment. Because these are things, which will constantly affect your daily agenda, obviously this is a passion that you've carried with you for years, and you've come to a point in your life where you realize it's now or never. These are the qualities and positive attitude that will bring that success home to you every time. There are people who wonder if they can do it and then there are people who just do it. They are the type of people who don't think twice and just move forward in the direction of their dreams. You know what your motivation is and you are the type of woman that handles your emotions in the right way. You already know that your mindset has more to do with where you're at and how you're going to get there.

Because I'm a Registered Nurse, I'll use the following example: A successful person can be anyone doing something extraordinary such as a young woman who wants to become a nurse when no one else in her family has achieved this status. She then enrols in a Health Sciences Program, commits to late study nights and no socializing. She completes it and graduates, but continual training and certification is still required to maintain proficiency. She may not be working independently, but she made sacrifices, and dedicated her time, energy, money, and focus to achieve her goal. She succeeded! The comparison can be made this way for any female in any career: certified training, degrees, time and commitment, sacrifice, focus, energy, dedication. When you make a decision and follow through, then it has to work for you because it fits the way that you see things. The end result is your victory. Such accomplishments are something that has to be seen with your own eyes and on your own terms. This is what it means to be an individual with a full life. It doesn't mean you have to make it on the cover of the business magazines. It just means you're striving to accomplish what you've dreamed of. When you think about how it translates in your life to be that successful business woman at that level of importance, where do you and your family fit in and where does your business training and social life co-exist? It's perfectly fine to not have all the answers at any given time.

Consider making a scale from one to five and arrange the people in your life in order of their importance to you. Where would you place yourself on that scale? Finding and maintaining balance in all areas of one's life is not impossible even for the high achiever. It all depends on your perspectives and where you place yourself in the big picture. There's only twenty-four hours in the day. How do you intend on creating the success that you desire? It's your dream that wants to come to life. Our situations change when we change the way we view them. If something has not worked one way, there are other routes to make it happen. By removing limiting beliefs that do not empower you, you're a step closer to the life you've always dreamed of. A great attitude will help you further along than you can imagine. Finally – Success – it's what you were made for.

Absolutely You Keys for Empowerment #13

Multi-tasking is a powerful skill that successful people excel at. In order to manage your life, secure your emotions first. Balancing life is an Attitude.

14 Love The Closed Doors in Your Life

Don't you just love it when things work out the way they're supposed to? Think about it for a second. It is either going to be good or bad whatever the outcome will be. So what would you rather go with? I'm the type of person who understands that things can go wrong, but NOW at this place in my life, I prefer to really think about it carefully.

I've always been an analytical individual. I don't accept things for face value. I know this is the result of my training as a nurse. Because I have learned through many of my own life experiences, those whom I am close to, and even my clients, that many times the doors that close in your life are a blessing in disguise. By having one door close, think of how much more room there is for you to NOW have the right door of opportunity open in your life. I have become aware that there is a process and it takes time to get from point A to point B. As long as we are positively focused, nothing can distract us from moving forward.

Sometimes I reflect on all the negative, painful, and hurtful things that I have experienced in life and realize that if I never had these experiences, I'm not sure I would have tried so hard to become better than I was at that point in my life. It's through all that discouragement, rejection, and hate that I found the courage to try harder and not give up so easily on myself. I decided that no one had the right to treat me badly. Because of my faith, I would never allow anger and resentment to consume me. People who I believed in had often disappointed me until I finally realized that I must start believing more in myself. I was often surprised how many times I met up with other people in my life who were also discouraged and hurt. This is why I choose to see the best in others and if they screw up, that's their problem. I'm not responsible for the actions and behaviours of others. We are each accountable for ourselves and the energy that we bring into the room. There are times in life that you may encounter people who feel that they have you all figured out and, instead of giving you the opportunity that you want, they turn you away. Be thankful that they did because if they could not appreciate the greatness that is within you, they would have tried to mess you up. You don't need this kind of jealousy and nonsense from people who have their own issues. Stay away from false prophets who will use every opportunity to woo you into believing in them, only to turn around and damage your precious emotions. The simple logic of any opinion is formed when a concept of unacceptable or acceptable theories is presented. I made a decision long ago to agree with the latter as the logic of unacceptable does not serve or benefit me and my values and self-confidence at all. This way if someone lets me down, I will not be concerned and distressed as it was not meant to be.

However, our human nature many times does pose a threat to this type of understanding especially if you do not take the time to question the other person's validity and commitment when others disappoint you. At moments of realization in any particular situation whether it is with a client or just myself, I can see how people choose to ignore the facts that give us clues to what the outcome of a situation may become. Some may see this as ignorance or even tolerance. What and how we decide to allow something to affect us identifies how we value ourselves in the big picture. This life that we live is all about us and how we choose to let things affect us at any given moment. We get to make all the decisions and choices that life brings our way. Sometimes we even have to build our own doors that never existed. It all starts with the way we view ourselves.

Every single moment that we experience is created by our preconceived ideas and our interpretation of how we choose to allow it to affect our lives. The mind's ability to be curious about our future experiences determines how we will react at any given time. Because we have that freedom to dream, we can create our future experiences before they happen. We can train ourselves to change our old reactions and behaviours and we can even convince our emotions to be shifted. An opportunity that never existed can be presented with the right intentions.

Your doors that were closed in the past belong where they are. You are a different person than the moment you experienced those past rejections. Your future is waiting and there are bigger doors of opportunities that you have been preparing yourself for. Our conscious decisions do affect our subconscious thoughts and patterns in life, whether we are aware of it or not. Every day that we are blessed with on this planet is a new beginning to another 24 hours. Ultimately everything we experience through our sensory perceptions and thought processes determines how we are progressing in life. Obviously, you can see I look at it from a scientific point of view as the whole world that exists before our very eyes is scientifically based and formed. Whether you choose to accept that or not is your choice as are all of the things in life to each and every one of us and it is yours to make the most of.

Absolutely You Keys for Empowerment #14

Life will always give you opportunities to grow and shine.
Not every door will lead you in the right direction.
Be grateful when you learn hard lessons
that keep you soft-hearted.
You are one of a kind, beautifully shaped and moulded
by all of life's lessons.
It's time to love the closed doors in your life.

15 Why Do You Care What They Think?

I believe that confidence is internally based on our perceived opinions of the environment around us. Everything we are exposed to in life either tests our abilities to grow stronger from them or shy away. We each have our own lives and based on my experiences and training, I have learned many things about confidence: how to gain it, how to learn from it through others, and how to deflect the things that destroy it. One of the biggest and most invisible challenges many people face is the question "What is my self worth?" Do you realize how special you really are when you make others feel good about themselves? Do you base your self worth on someone else's opinion of you? Thank you for being so caring and unselfish in your praise and appreciation of others.

Many people experience and may still be struggling with low self-esteem, lack of confidence, and fear of how others perceive them. I base this on several past conversations with my friends and clients who were walking through these issues, as well as what I've personally overcome. I'd love to say to everyone: "It's okay. Things will change and get better!" But I can't do that because I would be bluffing. The fact is, nothing changes unless we choose to change. We are the only ones who can change our perspectives and how we allow everything in our lives to affect us. If you feel like you have never been celebrated or appreciated enough, or even at all, for the things that you have accomplished and even conquered, now is the time to re-evaluate your whys.

We cannot please and make everyone happy. Often times, it is much better to just forgive and let go of the things that do not serve or empower us any longer. Sometimes the reasons may be unfair or inexcusable, depending on the circumstances or people who are in your immediate circle of closeness such as family or special friends. We cannot change who we are genetically related to. Because we are still connected to them in some way, we must make choices. Regardless of what the dynamics of your close circle of empowerment is and who they are comprised of, you can still learn to validate and appreciate yourself without their love, consent, or even approval.

Your life is all about you after all. It doesn't matter who your friends or family are. As we come to a place of self-awareness and confidence, our independence helps us understand and recognize who we are and see the value of our person. Overall, what really matters is what you think and how you feel about yourself. Many times, the people who are close to us and undervalue our self-worth are really the ones with the personal issues such as anger, jealousy, or even hatred. Please keep in mind this may have nothing to do with you at all. You must focus on your own dreams and live them passionately with a renewed perspective that there are many people out there waiting for you who already see your priceless and unique value while still celebrating and respecting you.

Stepping away from all forms of low vibration such as disrespectful attitudes and behaviours will bring much more empowerment and confidence in your life than you can imagine. So whether it is just a relationship or even a job where you feel under-appreciated or just tolerated, you must decide what your true worth is and how you want to show up in the world. Your self-love will cause you to attract the things that help you become your best possible self ever. Don't be so hard on yourself. Maybe you're going through life transitions such as empty-nest syndrome at home and changing dynamics between your spouse and yourself. You may have health issues or increased demands at work. Because you've always tolerated things a certain way or maybe you are not part of the inner "Gossip Circle," there is a good chance you have been carrying the extra baggage of negativity that's draining your zest for life. How about those community groups where you feel like an outsider trying to make yourself fit in by overextending your services and time? I've heard so many opinions about the feeling of inadequacy and how it affects a person's persona in such a sad, lonely, negative way. Unfortunately, these are the times many people shut themselves down and close off emotionally to the very ones who care about them. No man is an island and we all need to belong.

Life is very simple if we choose to look at it that way. Many people don't realize they have low self-esteem when they are struggling to acknowledge others. It does not indicate they are mean or selfish; it is just a way of holding onto what they think their value is. I can see how someone might feel intimidated and even have a hint of jealousy, but what these people don't realize is that when they themselves look past their own insecurities they can develop more as an individual and empower themselves in so many ways. Making powerful choices will get you where you need to feel appreciated and important because everyone is someone of great value. When you choose to let go of the harsh types of environments and the people who are part of them, you will feel like that baggage has been lifted off your life.

Doing this may be simpler than you even realize. It begins by changing your self-talk and increasing the love for yourself. Then with a renewed and enlightened perspective, you can discover new hobbies and try new and exciting things. Explore your world of unlimited potential, read more books, try creative activities or art classes, take self-development training, learn a new sport, acquire new job skills, continue with old forgotten hobbies, or how about getting a Life Coach to help you discover a whole new path of awareness. All of these suggestions that have been put aside or never thought of will empower and recharge any low self-esteem issues one may be facing.

When you set your intention to succeed in everything you do, you can't help but succeed. Is your focus on the goal and outcome or is it on what impact you want to make in your life? As you implement love as the strength of your journey, you will discover that love is such a powerful tool. The energy it emits only attracts more and more, and with the love of yourself, others, and the passion in your heart you can accomplish great and awesome things!

When life brings you so through so many storms, sometimes all you want is to do is relax and forget it ever happened and let it blow in the wind. But it's time to embrace the storms of life and understand how better you are for not letting it get the best of you.

By choosing not to forget the past for the wrong reasons in life, but acknowledging that you have learned how to be a better person despite circumstances, you are now much greater than ever because of it. Life has taught you to be a caring friend, a loving relative, a sincere neighbour, an honest worker, a dedicated partner and an amazing woman all around. You are only human because you choose to live your life without the limitations of regrets, heartaches, and tears. You are loved and accepted.

When we look at ways to bring more joy into our lives, we are growing, changing and living authentically. We find ourselves and increase our personal self worth and value by our increased confidence. Life is only a competition if you choose to look at it that way, or it can be an adventurous journey of self-development and accomplishments by goal-setting and personal growth. What we give we always get back; one of the many wonders of the Laws of Balance and Attraction. If you want to be recognized and appreciated more, then praise and validate others often. Don't worry about the focus being taken off of you. There is always someone who is observing your actions more closely than you think.

What you may not have thought of is that no matter where we are in our lives, we are an example to those closest to us and as we grow and develop our personal selves we have an audience who are emulating and growing as well. Make yourself a leader in your own eyes and then see how your self-worth and value is increased by your new perspective and positive attitude.

It's all about how you want to bring your value into who you want to be and then realizing it has nothing to do with what's going on around you as much as what's transpiring inside of you that counts. By making these simple decisions of restoring your self-worth with a renewed and empowered faith, the confidence of believing you are more than worthy to be appreciated brings out your fabulous self.

It will feel like cleaning your car windows and putting good fuel in your engine. You are in the driver's seat of your own life and how you choose where you want to go will get you there much sooner and happier.

Let go of the pain and give yourself a chance to heal. No matter what you do, life will still leave scars that you may still choose to forget. Find the strength and hope of living fully alive and healed from the things of the past, or what you are going through now. Let it go and BREATHE....

Keep looking for happiness and hope. God made you and God does not make junk. It all begins within your heart. What are you facing in your life that is making you give up so easily? You don't have to be anyone else. You don't have to have something special. You don't have to look a certain way. You don't even need to speak, dress, or walk like someone else.

You just need to believe in yourself. As a woman of greatness, you already have all you need to become the best you possible. That's right! Just believe in your dreams and let go of your failures, disappointments, and heartaches. I know it's not easy but I just want you to understand how special, unique, and important you really are! You are beautiful and smart. You are so special and you can be all that you want to be. Only you can do that!

This is for real and who cares what anyone else thinks.

Congratulations! You can now see more clearly with no distractions enroute to your destiny.

Absolutely You Keys for Empowerment #15

Live out loud!
Give yourself a chance to just be you.
There are days we can't be everything to everyone
and it's perfectly alright to find that time
where you can have your space and be yourself.
Love yourself for who you are.
Why do you care what they really think?

16 I'm a Motivator and Proud of It

I just wanted to share some of the reasons why I became a Registered Nurse and now a Big Vision Consultant. I have been through a lot of things in my life. Many of these experiences put me in a place where I constantly had to look within myself to find the answers to questions that I couldn't find elsewhere.

I know what it feels like to be hurt and have no one you can talk to because you feel so different. I can relate to what it feels like to not be like everyone else and that you don't belong. I even understand what it feels like when you think others may be laughing at you. I know what it feels like that you have something to say but no one wants or even cares to know. I know this and so much more....

Yes, I know this kind of pain; I lived it growing up. I overcame it. I embraced it and understood that these people who made me feel this way were the ones who were losing out. Now I am blessed to have so many great and empowering relationships with people of value and like-mindedness. I am still grateful for my past experiences in life. Not all of them were negative, but I understand the value of connection. I appreciate the collaboration of friends and having down-time. Just like everyone else, I love to be encouraged and supported through my goals and ambitions.

The more I think of this life, what can really be said of the infinite possibilities of love and encouragement?

Each day that we take a breath is a miracle of unlimited potential. Our dreams are alive as we allow them to live. What great aspirations are you letting go inside when you know very well the thoughts of success that are waiting for you?

As the only one who can make your hopes and determination something worth sharing with a world that is waiting for your genius to shine, it's time to let yourself out of the box to become who you really want from inside.

Forget those who don't comprehend the magnitude of your news.

There is something I must mention if you are a motivated person who goes after your dreams in life with zest and spontaneity. It's amazing how you still have to be aware of fake friends with smiles on their faces who will come along side of you and question your every move. Yet all the while they're just using you to enhance their own lives. Be careful of these individuals; they will make you feel like you're important until the next bus comes along.

You see, a highly motivated woman who has many roles and responsibilities is a rare quality and since women love to compete with each other this unfortunately is one of the roots of hate and jealousy. If you loved your friend or relative you would never try making yourself look better than them. Instead you would recognize the gifts they have and do your own thing.

If you are sincere you will build a solid foundation of trust that does not require you to be validated by everyone all the time. You have your amazing qualities just like them and you can develop yourself as well with your own ideas and gifts, trying not to compete and not being resentful if they do it first.

Unfortunately, on the road to success you may have to gauge how much you tell others about your goals, desires, and ambitions unless they have reciprocated equally.

It is not a fair exchange of responsibility in a friendship sadly to say. You are putting yourself at risk for being used, manipulated, or hurt. One of the ways you can learn to start protecting yourself in new friendships and relationships is to inquire about their past history.

You need to ask yourself if you want the baggage of someone else's broken and failed relationships in your life. Do you honestly have that kind of energy to keep fixing someone else's life? How are they going to treat you when they can't manage their emotions and lose it?

Obviously there are unresolved issues and their perspectives and outlook in life have been affected somehow. Right now you are looking really good as someone who has no problems and you would be a great person to unload on.

It's a sad thing when great relationships are damaged and even destroyed because of greed. Women have become so harsh at times that it takes away the beauty of who they are. Regardless of these experiences, I choose to forgive these people and release them. It's not my problem that they cannot see how they are devaluing themselves by their haughty nature.

Eventually it all catches up and they will be confronted with their own actions slapping them in their faces by someone else who is just as blind as they have been. I believe life allows us to repeat things until we figure it out or master ourselves with kindness, generosity, and love. I want you to know that you are somebody special.

You really need to understand that no one else can complete you. You see you were created in the image of perfection.

Your light is shining brightly wherever you are and it needs to shine brighter so you can feel the warmth of love's embrace. Don't worry about who doesn't love or like you. Please understand you really matter, and whatever you are walking through, you will have more of life to live and love it better.

No matter what you are thinking about right now, don't be discouraged any longer. You will have more time to live it, so please try to love and appreciate your life and all its blessings today, tomorrow, and forever.

Whatever you are feeling right now, make your thoughts and feelings lighter because you will have more moments to feel better than you are now. Your world is shaped by your words and thoughts; you are your own life's creator.

It's not relevant any longer what you think you may have done wrong. How bad can it be? Is there any true perfection in all the rest of humanity? Take a look at how far you have come and be grateful you will have more life moments to make things right. Some never had this chance, so life is showing you how you are blessed and that it doesn't love you any less.

You will always have the memories of what others said to you, talked about you, hurt or deceived you, but you don't need to let it overwhelm you any longer. You have more life to appreciate all those who never gave up on you, loved and always believed in you! You got this, what more could you ask for?

You see sometimes people judge you too easily because they see something that they wish they had in their own lives. Maybe it's something you didn't realize and comprehend. When you're too nice, it's hard to see who is a real friend. Your life is so precious because it's all about you and who you bring into it. Don't give up because a friend is always a friend and those who weren't are those who don't comprehend the greatness of the bond and what it holds till the end.

There are so many things that make you who you are. I encourage you to love yourself more and love those who love you. Forgive those who hurt you and don't forget those who forgave you. Never feel you have to work hard to be a friend or family because this life here on earth is what it is. Always appreciate those who appreciate you and learn to live and love again.

You see this world is very cold and lonely for those who are struggling in life. Never let emotions and life destroy what you have inside.

Instead be thankful even though some days are bad and some days make you so glad that you will forget all the things that have caused you disappointments in the past. Whatever the day, it's a new day you never had. Invest your love wisely and this will increase your faith, longevity, love, and confidence too.

I am always attracting beautiful people into my life with a genuine love for others who don't look at face-value but look at heart-value. People who are sincere and appreciative of relationships are motivating and thrive on building each other up.

These are the kind of values I myself have and love. I don't care for the competition and fake attitudes.

Life is a one way journey. It's about being there for one another; loving, forgiving, and building up.

Relationships should not be complicated. They should be honest, loyal, and sincere.

Our past does not dictate our future. It's supposed to propel us to strive more to achieve the things we want and make a difference.

As for my past experiences, I have forgiven and I have learned not everyone can appreciate you and can see things the way that you do. I have let go of those hurts and disappointments as it is a part of forgiveness. I hope that those people will come to understand they did not have the compassion and wisdom to see the value of who I was. They are the ones who I have forgiven and I can see that my strength is what has motivated me to continue on when others did not believe in me. By them rejecting me as part of their crowd, I had higher standards for myself.

I found inspiration in my dreams and looked outside my world to those who had overcome their own adversities and were scorned or even rejected. I motivated myself by understanding the value that I carried within myself. I looked at everyone as equal; I never judged or hated.

I was never jealous or envied another person. I spoke up for what I believed in, even when it was not received well by others. What mattered more was that it was received by people of integrity. I am so grateful that I did not grow up as a follower. I have seen and I have overcome. I am a motivator.

No one can be motivated unless they themselves are ready. Many people talk, but how much are they really doing?

Isn't it time to live the life you have wanted for so long? Forget about the talkers and the gossipers and the ones who never have anything good to say about you or your dreams and ambitions. Do they really matter in the BIG picture?

If someone really cares and believes in you for who you are, they will not compete, be jealous, or make your life miserable. They will just love you and everything about you.

Time to let go of all this nonsense and be who you are supposed to be. Stop listening to the negative people around you who don't really care about you.

Love yourself more to be all you are supposed to be... ONE Life and One Love. The world is waiting for you!

Absolutely You Keys for Empowerment #16

Live in love with yourself.
It's healthy to have self-love.
Take a moment to recognize the woman that you are in
this world. Many people know you but do you really
know who you are?
Self-awareness is a great place to evaluate
how you are showing up in the world.
By loving yourself more you help others to
love you for who you are as well.
I am a motivator and I am proud of it,
and you can be too!

17 Who Are You Going To Be Today?

The BEST way to feel good about yourself is to just decide to make it happen. Who ever thought it could be that easy as "Yes!" or "No!" You must decide how you want to feel since you always have a choice.

Do you want to feel good and accept yourself for who you are? Do you need to forgive yourself for something you need to address in your life? It's time to finally let go of all the expectations and guilt of the past.

You can give yourself the chance to make a new start by giving yourself permission to move on and make a new change in your life.

No one is perfect and no one has all the answers in life, we are all here just making choices every minute of every hour. What we become is a result of who we choose to be, minute by minute, second by second.

Have you ever seen an onion full of thick and thin layers? If you have peeled back the thin skin, you would know that it is simple and yet complicated. Then when you break through the layers upon layers, the onion juice makes your eyes water.

Well, we are like an onion. YES!! ...believe it, we are: The layers represent our lives. They tell our stories. As the layers are thick, so are the experiences we have walked through. Then we have our moments: the emotional tear jerking, struggles, hardships, heart breaks. As we grow emotionally, we can see more layers and we can see more tears.

Life is not easy. It is a blessing indeed. But, everyone has their own personal struggles and pain they must endure. No one is immune to this thing called life and all its diversities. We are all connected by birth, marriage, occupation, gender, ethnicity, geography, education, religion, politics, economics, health, and history.

As we develop as a society we are all affected by what is happening on the world front. We can deny many things, but one thing we cannot deny is that life happens in layers: birth, toddlerhood, childhood, adolescent, teenage, young adulthood, middle-aged and senior adulthood. Throughout these life-cycles we develop layers of experiences like onions. We grow and express ourselves while learning the whole time. We continue developing creatively and into our unique selves. As we go through our own family process, have children, take care of them, teach them and watch them grow up themselves, we then continue evolving as a result of our lived experiences.

As these physical changes and life cycles continue, we also go through many diverse experiences. Many will have endured the hardships of job losses, losing loved ones, relocating, marriages and divorces, failures and disappointments. We sometimes share our emotions with those who we are close to or anyone who relates to our stories.

As an "Onion" person, we need to understand that with each experience we go through it becomes part of our own personal development. We have always been able to choose what type of person we want to become. So continue being that onion but let your layers bring out the best in you. Don't let it bring tears to your eyes when you look back, but let it bring tears to someone else's eyes because of what you have been through and survived.

Many people will try to paint you with one brush thinking you are just like everyone else. How sad for them, not even comprehending the journey you have been on to become your very best. When this happens you know it is their loss if they can be so careless and not see the reality before their eyes. Never let it undervalue who you are and what you have been through. The truth of the matter is that no one is alike and no one can be something they are not. Many may try to pretend to be something they are not, but true integrity comes from within and only if you are listening to your heart and following your intuition can you clearly see the difference between what is for real and what is not.

When you get dressed up, don't forget to bring your blessings wherever you go. Take a moment and share it with the world around you. Spend an extra second giving a warm smile and saying "Thank you" or even "Excuse me" to the person you want to squeeze by.

Try holding that door open or giving the parking spot you have been waiting patiently for to the next car that comes along. How about giving the extra change someone is short on in line? Another way to share your blessings is to check your food pantry every once in a while and fill a box up to drop off at the local food bank. Donate regularly to your homeless shelter and drop off extra clothing for the men and women who need a little something more. When we live in the confidence that we are so blessed and have so much already that we cannot contain it within ourselves, you never know, we may end up receiving more to keep on Blessing.

Sometimes there are things in life that need addressing as they may be conduits of negativity that drain your positive energy. Are you still attached to someone or something, but not aware of it? We leave so many doors open from our past that we forget we are still connected with the pain. Past relationships gone bad and other events or experiences that you have forgotten about may still be associated with you. In any case it's time to let these things go. Anything which no longer serves or empowers you as a person of value and integrity must be released for you to be free. Close the doors that are leaking the past into your life presently. Doing so will ensure that you are NOT losing something valuable such as your laser focus, ingenuous creativity, unlimited energy, and fabulous freedom.

Some journeys make you weary while others make you fierce. Walking through these moments can swiftly change your mind about life and all it entails. But when you have matured in all your facets and understand that it's not all about you, your integrity is established as you have earned life's scars and have walked through your own pain. It may have taken a while for your wisdom to mature to understand that life is not a competition. Instead it is a compliment to the lives we have selectively been introduced to along our own personal journey.

Just picture what it might be like one day realizing that all the people we may have hurt, offended, or disrespected for whatever reasons was only a test! Envision if you were actually walking through a major exam on the highest level of spiritual leadership or something very significant. Imagine if the thoughts we hold against others deep in our hearts are the compass of what direction our life prospects may be? We think the dreams, goals, and successes here on this planet are the things to strive for.

But what if we are all connected together? Visualize there is a higher power – God. Some say there is an omnipotent entity that is overseeing our very thoughts, actions, attitudes, behaviours and is well aware of our motives at all times. What would you do differently if you knew?

Believe it or not I am thankful for all those people who have actually hurt me in the past by their selfish ways, deceitfulness, jealousy, or manipulation. No one is perfect. I have released them all to their own ways. I also love them because they need to be loved. I have learned that I am not perfect either and have made my own share of mistakes.

I am now attracting more powerful and positive relationships into my life. Because I have learned to recognize that hurting and broken people create more brokenness and hurts, this is the reason I have always chosen to forgive. I have even asked forgiveness many times when it was not necessary on my part. It wasn't always easy but I learned that I must also forgive myself for allowing myself into situations and holding back my peace through unforgiveness. I have come to appreciate that had it not been for the wickedness or hurtful ways of others, I would not have learned or managed to become stronger and wiser for it.

Life is not always a basket of roses. There are many thorns along the way as well. I have already learned that the very people who you think would love and support you, can and will let you down. It doesn't matter who they are. Family and friends are just people. If they don't have your heart and love you for you are, it will be revealed in certain behaviours and actions against you. Our Universal Laws are amazing how they show up this way. Don't fret. Just let people be. Forgive and release them. We each have our paths to walk. Make yours pleasant and loving.

Sometimes the people you expect to support you will let you down. Don't expect because you have paid into something or belong to an organization, that they care when they will only look out for their favourites because they can and maybe because no one points it out. If they don't have integrity to act accordingly, it's not your job to correct them. One day their ways will become exposed. After all, it's the Universe's job to maintain balance on our planet Earth. All things living are accountable to contributing to this balance of the Universe.

Our lives depend on the blessings of God and His Universal Laws which are fantastic and benefit our greatest good if we learn to use it wisely. This is the reason it's wise to not waste your energy on negative and draining relationships. Release them and let them go. Even the people you freely support, motivate, and encourage may turn against you because they think they found something better or maybe they just never really cared. Let them go!

I'm telling you from my own experiences, our perceptions are limited by the capacity of our heart-centered love. Universal Laws are powerful this way. They create balance in our lives.

It's all about the energy we choose to keep or discard. This energy will attract more of itself to your world. Don't worry; choose to let all the negativity go especially if it is hurting you in any way. Your life and its life force need to be healthy and burden free. You will experience more joy and love through your raised vibration of Love. It's not until you mindfully choose to live in love and forgiveness that you begin to continually release the pain which you recognize without hesitation is a God-given ability you have inside. You are a person of compassion and you will start to appreciate the gifts inside of you.

Love is much more than it first appears. It gives you super human strengths that you could never do without.

Love can make the most horrible of experiences become a mere scar of an event. Love is the most priceless and powerful energy and is highly sought after. It can instantly change the biggest storms into a beautiful sunlit day. Love is irreplaceable just like you. There is an unlimited abundance of love waiting for you and it is all about you. You are the Universe of your own world. God loves you and I love you just as you are.

Once you clear away what you attracted into your life from the yesteryears and forgive yourself, you can start attracting the positive, healing, and supportive relationships that you need more of in your life today. You are that powerful!

It's always a good idea to become the person you know you were born to be. Keep in mind that the best comparison, if you must, is to only compare yourself with who you were yesterday. Your true value increases better that way.

Who are you going to choose to be today?
Be the Onion you were born to be! Be You!

Absolutely You Keys for Empowerment #17

Live as the leader in your life.
Take inventory of all the decisions you have made
in the last several months and determine
if you were satisfied with the outcomes.
Now you can see yourself as someone
who is in total control of making choices that
attracts exactly what you desire.
Who are you going to be today?

18 The Value of Your Opinion

The best way to feel good about you is to just do so. Whoever thought it could be that easy? Don't you love when someone's opinion of you isn't the most important thing anymore? I'm learning what really matters more are actually what I choose NOT to let into my world.

When people think they are a gift to others or believe they have higher value, that's when their real personality and worth comes through. I've learned through many experiences the way to see a person is through the motives of their heart and to honestly look at the lives in which they have interacted with. There should be diversity, depth, and devotion as well as dedication to each relationship. By understanding myself more, I've seen the many ways people can be caring, loving, cruel, or even hurtful. This validates why not all lessons in life are pleasant.

However, when walking in the midst of a storm, you can't always see the end in sight. But you know and believe it will not last forever. Because of this you know one day, one hour, or one moment, if you wait a little longer, your answer will come. Life is a great teacher in herself. Sometimes she's hard and sometimes she's tender. It's the bittersweet moments that can be the hardest because we are constantly trying to figure our lives out.

Why does it have to be this way? Why can't things be different? When will it ever make sense? Take a deep breath and thank "GOD" for the times you "coulda, woulda or shoulda" because now that you are where you're at, you can approach those moments and discover something about yourself you never knew before. Maybe you didn't try because it was not the right time for you. Now that you've lived through what you have, what you will do?

Once you know in your heart the value and courage you have gained so far in your life, you will always have more substance to reflect on because of your own personal experiences. This will bring you a richer more satisfying life with depth, devotion, and dedication. Your confidence in yourself will be so strong. You will not be looking around for the causal compliments to boost your ego anymore.

A life that has experienced much diversity will possess more value and give more to others because of what it has walked already through. You need to see the importance of YOUR own value. Your opinion makes your life unique and inspires those around you.

For those of you who are still struggling with things people have said to you past or present, and you don't know how to react or approach the situation, this is for you. Many times you may not even realize things are hurtful at the very moment they happen.

Here are some simple steps to remember:
First of all, forgiveness is a big thing. It helps you to calm down and think clearly. Also understanding that you have so much control of your life will help you look at things from a different point of view.

Secondly, don't let ANYONE speak against you. Don't accept it or receive it into your heart, spirit, mind, or body and never encourage anyone to power trip you no matter who they are and regardless who has more title, experiences, finances, etc. YOU are made to live the life of your dreams and to possess your destiny filled with passion. You are meant to be purpose-driven and your special and unique gifts were originally created to fit ONLY you! When you keep these simple methods of approaching uncomfortable situations in the future you will see the increased confidence you have by the way you begin to process things differently from now on.

I have such an overwhelming sense of gratitude in my heart for this thing we call daily living. Our lives are such a beautiful thing full of so many wonderful and amazing events.

Our prayers are answered continually and our mistakes forgiven. Every moment we breathe and have emotions is a miracle in itself. How can it be explained other than something of immeasurable love and wonder that you have all that and so much more to enjoy?

Live your life with the wonder of gratitude for the health, wealth, and blessings that it is. Give without regrets. Forgive and forgets. Love unconditionally. Trust with childlike faith. Many will not forget. Life is a gift. Be careful with your words and what they create.

Some people give up before they have even lived. Don't be like the walking dead. Live your life like it's supposed to be, with the conviction and passion to be appreciated and enjoyed. Give it all you've got. My beautiful angel daughter never had the chance that you do and so it is with many others who had wished they had only one more day in this world to make a difference in their lives. Live abundantly in the knowledge and peace of the love that comes from wisdom and greater understanding of your self-worth.

Because you are a gift to those who love and adore you just as you are, you don't need a boyfriend/girlfriend or significant other to bring value and make your life complete. You just need your unconditional love for yourself to understand how much your creator and loved ones want for you. Imagine how your future self needs you to make a difference right now.

Life happens to everyone and many times the scars are so deep within the soul. As human beings, the greatest misconception we perceive is not realizing how we can affect each other. So my dear friends treat each other the way that you want to be treated and let go of who and what no longer serve to empower or bless you. Be healthy in your whole life for your whole life.

Stay blessed. All that you need will come in perfect time when you are ready to receive it.

Absolutely You Keys for Empowerment #18

Live in humility and grace. No one likes to be around
anyone who is proud or obnoxious.
Your value in the eyes of your peers will increase
because your attitude towards others is sincere.
You are a beautiful and sexy woman.
Live to create change in your world.
You are the center of your Universe.
Everything revolves around your expectations
and actions. However, change must first
begin within you.
Let it begin with the value of your opinion.

19 The Sweetest Things

Sometimes the sweetest things you can do for others are just being sincere and polite. Believe it or not, we have a very troubling society that is unlearning a basic etiquette in life which our parents and grandparents lived by. We need to care more and realize that our lives are not all about us. We affect one another on a grand scale. Every word spoken is just as important as every word that is left unspoken. Thoughts and behaviours have energy attached to them. Consider the energy you bring into a room or conversation. How much more the effect from an interaction where you may have disregarded another's feelings?

Many people are already immune to the fact that it is not proper to just be silent. Since when has it ever been acceptable to give a gift and not be thanked by the recipient? Or how about allowing our kids to be rude to others or disrespectful to their elders? This is all the same thing. Lack of respect is a slow poison to humanity. People thrive on positive reinforcement and love. Respect others and you will be respected back, no questions asked. Thankfully there are still individuals who operate in a state of Gratitude and Appreciation as they are aware of the Universal Laws of Blessings. These individuals have integrity. We all want to be associated with people like these as we are all equal and valuable.

When we are moving in the high frequency vibration of Love we attract more of it around us. As this continues we automatically let go of things that are not in the same vibration. Allow things to depart that go against your true nature, especially if they conflict with your integrity and values. By releasing these hindrances, you are at the same time allowing in the right things that resonant with your core. Everyone loves to feel good, and everyone loves to be treated with respect, including you and me.

To activate more good things and positive experiences in your life simply show love and gratefulness for each and every person you meet in life. If you know people you just ignore, consider asking yourself why? You are blocking blessings in your own world. It's not difficult to be a person of kindness or integrity. Just start by saying "Thank you," "You're Welcome!" or "I appreciate you!" Do it frequently! But be ready to start feeling increased love, happiness, and joy in your life.

You might become so delighted by the positive shift of vibration in your life that you begin to randomly speak and do good things for others. You may find yourself complimenting someone for something you notice about them. You may start to go out of your way to be nice to everyone. You may begin to smile more often. Believe it or not, you may even start treating everyone equally. As you treat others better, your world shifts in many ways. We are spiritual beings in a physical world.

Sometimes you discover that people are not all that you though them to be. People have ways of showing their true colors sooner or later. Does that mean you have a reason or even a right to react and put them in their place?

People believe they have a right and obligation to themselves and even others to stand up and speak out. I am not telling you what you must do in your life, but I do want to address the consequences of what could happen if you always react and take things into your hands. The circumstances could be emotionally charged and affecting you directly, or not even disturbing you at all but you decide to fix the problem anyways. You see, life has many facets and so do people. People are not perfect and neither is life. Does it justify that you step up and let others hear what you have to say? Ask yourself what the outcome would be for you and your loved ones? Is your emotional reaction going to heal or help anyone? These are all very important and valid questions.

Think of the outcome. Are you guaranteed it will benefit you and you will get a favourable response from your offender and someone who has crossed the line? With any situation, there is always a protocol how things are moderated so you do have an equal opportunity to speak your feelings. Do you want to keep attracting more and more complicated issues? If you don't want the extra stress consider stepping back and assessing the situation. Re-frame your experience.

I recall speaking with a colleague who told me about a business association she was formerly connected with. The members felt that they could use her material and even her tagline to support their brand. She was appalled and shocked. We discussed this situation and with the outcome she realized they could not copy her vision. Ironically, they didn't even understand the meaning of her material. Unfortunately these people didn't understand the wrong kind of attention they were giving themselves. On a grandeur scale, my colleague was happy realizing that she did not want to attract anymore nonsense from amateurs into her own life and business. She set her intention to step up her own vision and successfully left them in the dust-storm of her success! I am so proud of my friend.

Allowing yourself to be grateful for the things that come into your life, as a magnet for success, because you have focused on higher level energy thinking automatically deflects lower level negativity. This helps you recognize what is draining and consuming as a destructive force to your success and unlimited potential in life.

You will find in life that not everything you do will first start out how you want. Maybe the communication went out the window, or maybe you never saw the whole picture as it was presented. Relax and breathe again!

Life is a learning adventure. Once you get a hold of your dream, plans, and intentions, these things will reorganize together the way they were meant to be. Just inhale energetic positivity and exhale draining negativity. Love the process; it is making you sharper and more focused on what you are all about.

Take time to count the blessings in your life. Every moment we take time for the little things, we create a positive blanket of love surrounding us. We are more than just ourselves. The people we are connected to bring out many qualities in us such as being supportive, caring, forgiving, honest, genuine, patient, and understanding, even when we screw up. We are all on a one way journey and no one is greater than the other. Everyone counts and it takes many experiences along our way to help us bring out the best possible person we can become. Be grateful when things happen at that moment, otherwise it could have turned into the worst outcome of our lives. Everyone is limited only by the number of days we carry forth, yet at the same time these days can possibly be extended by the amount of love that we apply to them. Count your blessings and identify each one of them by name.

You can increase your faith and make your life more significant. If you add value to everything you do, things will automatically take on a whole new dimension. By believing in yourself and what you want in your life, blessings will come out of nowhere. Increase your faith in others. It's not the same as trusting, but it's just acknowledging that you have confidence things will work out the way they're supposed to into something BIGGER. Allow yourself to trust the process of whatever you are walking through. It doesn't mean that you don't care what happens. It just means you won't allow yourself to get bent out of shape any longer. Increase your faith and see what miracles can take place in your life.

So many people will drift through your life for various reasons. It may be that you have grown and they just can't keep up or they have moved in another direction that fits their personality and passions better. This is all good because you don't want anyone slowing down your evolution and progress.

Let them go. Allow yourself the space to refresh your perspectives so the right people can see you more clearly. They are the ones who you need around as you step into your Destiny of Greatness!

You're shifting upwards in your life. This is your sign of Success!

Absolutely You Keys for Empowerment #19

Live your life as a healer.
Everything painful you have experienced up to this point
can be healed by simply choosing to forgive and release.
Life is beautiful. These are the sweetest things.

20 Success Comes After Failure

Have you ever tried something and been unsuccessful at the 1st or even 2nd attempt? If this happened to you, it doesn't mean that you're a failure or have no value to offer others. In fact, it means you ARE a creative genius with so much potential waiting to be released to the world.

Disappointments actually confirm that it was not the right moment in your life's journey to make such a thing pay off. Your so-called setbacks in life are valuable pieces of information that you can learn so much more about yourself and the world around you, should you choose to allow it. Sometimes things don't proceed because you're not in the right place in your life to carry it through as well as you should.

So don't be hard on yourself for your obstacles or let downs. They are intricate pieces of your life's work. After all, it was meant to turn out the way it did so you could re-evaluate your perspectives and grow from it. Nothing worth gaining ever had a few resources to establish or grow from.

Ever feel like no one cares? Have you been stuck with the biggest job ever and others will benefit from your hard work? Sometimes you have to remember that everything comes back to you in one way or another.

What goes around always comes back around. Treat everyone the way that you want to be treated. Not everyone knows the whole story so please remember that you have a right to live without limitations. Stop worrying about people who don't care about you anyways. The biggest shortcoming of the nicest people in the world is the sadness placed on them by simple and stupid rejection. You are a work in progress whether you realize it or not. Everything priceless was less valuable at some point until the time was right for it to be recognized as a treasure worth cherishing.

I have often thought about how everyone needs a special kind of break-away from the busyness in their lives. It's not easy when you have a full schedule. So many of my colleagues make excuses from doing the things they should, not because they want to, but because many times they need to maintain their sanity and peace of mind.

Our lives get so overwhelmed that we forget to keep a balance of work and play with the VIP (very important people) people in our lives. It's disrespectful and sometimes heartbreaking when we forget how important these relationships are to us. They were there for us from the start and have always been our most loyal companions and support system. In my own experience, I have often witnessed that if someone keeps neglecting their own needs and desires to be heard and appreciated, eventually their zest and passion for life gets burned out.

I encourage you to make time for healing moments. It's necessary to maintain balance and keep your personal relationships in check by scheduling time for you and those who are valuable to you. If you are neglectful, it will take more time later on to resolve it if you can. The investment you make now will give you years of added interest from the ones you love and cherish. Your relationships contribute to who you are.

You can only be happy if you are happy. There is no alternative to contentment. Be real and be content. There is always a balance. Being a statistic is not cool anymore. So, if you have had issues in your relationships, there's still time to heal them. You are a success so start living it in every area of your life. Otherwise it will only contradict your words.

Appreciate your life and all its personal moments. These support who you eventually become. Whenever you may feel a disconnection with your divine purpose in life, I encourage you to seek out that which brings satisfaction to your spirit, mind, and body. It is easier to realign your dimensions equally with very simple steps, than to forever search for a solution to your discontent.

Preferred ways of soul satisfaction and divine purpose discovery include physical exercise, healthy and healing lifestyle changes, rest and relaxing more often, passion and romance, simple or skilled hobbies, interaction with nature, reading, writing, drawing or painting, praying, and mediation.

I have personally observed that any form of arts and crafts that allow your creative force to shine through is quite satisfying. Sometimes just watching movies and getting caught up with a part of your life that has been put aside for too long is a secret key to being stress-free.

Our close relationships are also a good source of inspiration. Assess your satisfaction levels in life routinely, if not daily. Doing so will help you to consciously choose that which attracts the most fulfilled and happy life. You will never be far from what your divine life's purpose is. Your spirit, mind, and body know you better than you realize. Help yourself to be in alignment always.

Let go of all your failures and start learning from them. It's time to stop carrying around the baggage of past difficulties. Why do you want to keep tormenting yourself?

There is no justification for you allowing this kind of misery in your own world. You are an amazing person. You are creative and kind. You light up the room when you walk into it. You make others smile. Your laughter is contagious.

Why do you want to hold on the past failures any longer? A personal prison of pain is not cool! Let it go! Give yourself the chance to be better, do better, and feel better!

You are more than able my friend. Don't give up so easily. Look how far you have come already. Everyone has a journey, although not everyone is aware of their progress at given time.

Let your light shine so others can find their way back home. We all need guidance at some point or another. Your greatest moment is realizing you need direction and are humble and willing to receive that which can make the biggest shift worthwhile.

Your Success is in your Steps!

Are your steps lining up with your big picture vision? Do you have a game plan in place? What are your set-back plans? Do you praise yourself enough if you accomplish something that actually fits into your big plans?

"What if's" are holding you back in life, especially if you always allow them to affect your motivation, mood, and attitude. Consider how well you handle personal praise or rejection. Do you bounce back easily?

Remember that your success is all in your strategy and how you follow through. Everyone's steps to success are different because we are all different! This makes you one in a million or billion. You were and are a success story the day you entered into this plane of existence on your Birthday. Congratulations! Your life is unique and interesting and will still resonate with others who relate to similar events or life experiences.

Remember is that each individual's personal story has value and with that comes priceless knowledge and insight that may possibly be the very thing you need to hear.

It's not over till it's over. Live your life with love and gratitude. Don't make the holidays the only time you are nice and kind to others. Your intentions will always show. Your life is an opportunity to live, excel, and improve every day. You create your life by the thoughts of your success or failures. Choose to live without regrets.

Love yourself more. You are a BIGGER success because you are a conqueror. You are a Winner and you are loved, just the way you are!

Absolutely You Keys for Empowerment #20

Live to give love and acceptance to others.
Begin your day with pure love and bliss
towards yourself. Then you will see yourself as an
ambassador of love.
As you embrace the love that is within you,
Everything that once let you down or disappointed you,
including yourself
becomes a ladder of lessons to climb.
Success comes after failure.

21 Overcoming Rejection with Grace

How many times have you personally faced rejection? It's never a pretty sight and you always feel like crap. So what do you do to get over the sting? Rejection comes in every shape, size, and form and you can't always avoid it. Sometimes it's so smooth and subtle that you don't realize it's happened until the ship has sailed on. This could be the worst experience because you never even saw it coming. Maybe you're the type of woman who ignores all the warning signs even though the flags are flapping wildly in the wind.

You choose to be optimistic and open-minded because you're such a good person. So why would anybody in their right mind hurt you just like that?

People think rejection really has nothing to do with who they are, but more often than not it is based on any of the following reasons:

1. They got what they wanted from you.
2. You freely gave them what they wanted.
3. They didn't appreciate your value.
4. You don't see your own value.
5. You're too nice or naïve.
6. You're insecure or lack confidence.
7. You live in fear.
8. You're a follower.
9. You're too smart for your own good.
10. You're too pretty

11. You're too generous
12. You don't want to be alone.
13. You think you have to fit in.
14. You let them take advantage of you.
15. You're too quiet and don't speak up.
16. You're not happy.
17. You're too trustworthy.
18. You haven't found your purpose or discovered your passion in life.
19. You've been rejected before and expect rejection again.
20. You expect to be used.
21. You have destructive self-talk.
22. You don't love yourself.
23. You're not satisfied with life.
24. You're bitter and angry.
25. You try too hard.
26. You ignored the warning signs again.

Let's face it, if any of these things resonated with you at one point or another in your life, you more than likely attracted that inevitable rejection. I'm not saying that it was entirely your fault. What I'm strongly suggesting though is if your frame of mind was drifting along any of these paths, you contributed to the negative energy that you brought into that relationship.

According to the Law of Attraction, anything that is of low vibration is negative and automatically interrupts the frequency of positive vibrations. Thoughts, coupled with emotions, are very powerful and will continue attracting exactly what it is to where it is unless the thoughts and emotional energy change.

I encourage everyone to use the following "Rejection Quiz" on a regular basis. As a Life Coach, I have used many systems for assisting my clients to manage their own lives. This is a guide that I have developed specifically geared towards rejection.

REJECTION QUIZ

1. Did I deserve this to happen to me?
    Yes or No
2. Did I see it coming?
    Yes or No
3. Did I ignore the warning signs?
    Yes or No
4. Why did I ignore them?
    I didn't want to believe it.
    I wanted it to go away.
5. Can I fix it?
    Yes or No
6. Why should I fix it?
    They're making a mistake letting me go.
    I didn't give them a real chance to know me.
7. Can I do better?
    Yes or No
8. What's stopping me from doing better?
    I didn't think I could.
    How would I do it?

The intention of this quiz is NOT to determine a score of your level of rejection, but to actually bring an awareness of how rejection can affect your overall perceptions about your life.

Once you have completed the quiz, I would like to expand on each of these specific questions and answers. For those of you who are exploring this quiz, these are my professional opinions based on all my training.

1. **Did I deserve this to happen to me?** Of course not! You're an amazing woman with so much potential

inside and are so much better than you give yourself credit for. So why would you even think that way? You know very well it's time to start believing more in yourself.

We have covered confidence and self-esteem already in previous chapters, so here is something else to think about. Is it possible that you've actually gotten comfortable with allowing the "pity party" to continue and because it's what you are familiar with, it's now become your comfort zone?

I have worked with clients and colleagues who are attracted to this kind of drama. You see, rejection can actually stir up a special type of reaction that far too many of my peers have observed in their own lives until they finally recognized how crippling it really was. Trust me when I say this. I am well aware that some people allow rejection to happen because they have such low-self esteem. It is far easier and safer to wait for rejection than to strive harder, step out, and take the risk of finally being satisfied despite all the land mines they may encountering along the way. They will not even entertain the thought of happiness and contentment in life.

We are all familiar with the group of females who love to share their sad stories with one another and in doing so they verbally bash their offenders and continue attracting these experiences back into their lives. And so the cycle repeats. The bottom line - you don't deserve this to happen to yourself and until you accept this into your life, things may never change like you would want them to.

2. **Did I see it coming?** If you actually saw some form of rejection coming into your life, you should understand why you didn't try to prevent it from taking place. No matter what happens in life, we cannot change the past. Because we have prior experiences logged into our

internal hard-drives we have access to detailed memories on demand. We can recall the smells, sights, and sounds of so many experiences that our brains are capable of effortlessly recalling these events and playing them back for us in such an amazing way. We can even add specific outcomes to those memories if we want to, therefore enhancing the experiences further. Wow!

We do indeed have very spectacular and intricate minds. So I often wonder why we choose to make our lives more complex than they really need to be. You have your emotional connection to past experiences and you remember what happened leading up to a similar experience because hindsight gives us an advantage in the future. If we really want to utilize the knowledge we already possess, based on our past experiences, it will help us to potentially avoid heartaches and disappointments as we learn how we can respond or behave differently should similar events occur.

It's time to stop letting yourself down any longer. You are the only one responsible for your actions as well as reactions, especially if you can understand how important of a role you play in your own happiness and success.

3. **Did I ignore the warning signs**? First of all you have to acknowledge that you have been ignoring the warning signs all along. Then ask yourself why you may have chosen to avoid them altogether. Let's begin to explore if there is some way you can stop this destructive low-self esteem cycle from carrying on in your life. It's like the familiar saying that goes, "You can't keep repeating the same thing and expect to get different results."

When it's your happiness and success we're talking about, you have to determine where you place yourself in the big picture. Many people may not even realize they have control over their own outcomes. They settle easily and avoid conflict at all costs. This does not mean one should expect conflict, but rather it is a common behaviour by many who have been rejected to simply neglect their value and place low standards on themselves.

Fear is a substantial factor that many women feel. For instance, they may dread being singled out because they are so outspoken or fear the humiliation of being told negative things about themselves. Another common fear is losing something such as role in an unbalanced personal or business relationship. The saddest part of all this is that the outcome will not be as horrible as they may think.

When you have the courage to speak up and share your insights, most people are very receptive and understanding. You are in this relationship because you are already valued and cared for. Focus on the positive benefits of being honest and sharing your feelings instead of living secretly in the fear of the unknown. When you imagine a positive response and embrace the emotions that go with it, you are sending a request to the Universe for something beautiful. You are inspiring yourself to believe that nothing is impossible for you to receive into your life.

4. **Why did I ignore them?** Most women are guilty of this at one time or another. It honestly does not matter who you are and what you do for a living. It is a variable in the journey of life that constantly presents itself to us, and based on what we are doing at that exact moment in time, we decide if we want to acknowledge or pursue it regardless of the benefits. This does not mean you are unsuccessful or negligent in your life's affairs. It just means there can be moments of overwhelm coupled with all of the various life issues and responsibilities concerning ourselves and those

close to us. It just becomes an overload of responsibilities that may easily be overlooked. Stop feeling guilty and take mental notes to reach out towards the other person sooner. There is absolutely nothing wrong with checking in and asking if things are where they should be at your end. Spend time getting to know each other and be real. Every relationship should have some standard of expectations just as you should have for the other person, whether this is a close friend or relationship. Communication is vital for the survival of any relationship.

5. **Can I fix it?** It always takes two to make a relationship work. You can try your hardest but at the end of the day, if it's not working then it's time to release it and let it go no matter how painful. Losing a friend or significant other because of the fallout in a relationship is very similar in terms of emotional trauma. Intimacy has occurred because you have bared your soul and shared parts of your intellectual self that were considered special and unique to you.

6.

Rejection of this nature is tragic and can leave a person feeling numb and unable to trust anyone again for quite some time. It also prevents anyone from getting close to you. When you have built up internal walls of protection, not everyone will understand your reasons and not everyone will actually care to even try. For this reason, you must determine in your heart if this person is worth your time and effort to try harder and give more of yourself, even with the possibility of being rejected all over again.

The interesting thing about rejection is that everyone experiences it and while some may be more open to speaking about the hurts and disappointments from previous relationships, not everyone wants to share and be so vulnerable. They may need their own space and time to heal properly to be able to give you what you deserve.

Two hurting people cannot help each other. Everyone has to journey through life individually. Your baggage is different than theirs, so you must process your own issues alone. You have to understand if you are seeking a relationship to heal yourself or are actually ready to give all of yourself completely with no hidden fear and rejection coming with you.

The shadow of fear may eventually overtake many things in your relationship causing you to step away from the life you truly desire and when it happens it may come across the wrong way and give mixed messages to those you are closest to. At this point you will have to really face things whether you want to or not.

7. **Why should I fix it?** Not everyone likes confrontation. Even at the best of times, because there is so much happening in a person's life, misunderstandings happen far more frequently than they should. Yet there is always a diplomatic and peaceful way to approach these conflicts in one's life without coming across too opinionated or outspoken and still get your message across. Maybe you believe your feelings have been neglected and overlooked and you have held back your true thoughts and ideas.

As already mentioned, only you can determine your worth and value. The higher the value you place on yourself, the more you will want to make things work or else you would not have entered into this relationship to begin with whether as a friend or significant other. You have already committed yourself to being faithful and loyal and you can see how this relationship compliments you in so many ways. Therefore it is not a question if you should try, but actually how can you fix it and make it work. While I cannot tell you what you should do, you already know many different ways that make this person feel appreciated and loved. Now consider their personal morals and things that they appreciate.

I don't know the details of your situation or if you are actually facing a situation of this nature right now, but I can say that because every relationship is a two way streak and communication is a very powerful tool. This is a great way to make an effort instead of suffering needlessly. At least you have given it a fair chance to mend and make it better, if this is what the other person wants as well. There is a unique way to approach sensitive situations without causing more distension. Consider asking the other person how they feel. Let them explain themselves fully and if you still don't get a proper response or the answers you're looking for, ask specifically what you could do better? Be prepared to hear things about yourself that you may not agree with right away. Take detailed notes but don't be offended. Then ask this person if they are willing to help you make these changes. Remember, if this relationship is valuable to you it should be to them as well. Also, this is the ideal time to talk about why it was never brought up before.

Be calm again and learn about yourself. It will be quite an enlightening moment. There are no guarantees it will work out as you expect but communication is powerful if you remove the emotional attachment to the actions and reactions. With a clear mind you may see something you never noticed before.

8. **Can I do better?** You'll never know if you can do better in anything unless you try. "Doing better" is based on an individual's perception of themselves and what level of satisfaction they are in at that present

moment in their lives. So let me ask you this; are you currently satisfied with your life? When we assess this awareness in detail, we can then determine what exactly is making you feel this way. It may be any number of things or it might be just one particular issue that is affecting everything else around you. So when you have looked at this carefully, you can then shift your thoughts into addressing WHAT exactly you can do to make things better to bring about the satisfaction and happiness you so desire in life.

The bottom line is that we can all do better and we have consistently proven this theory on a daily basis. What we were once amateurs in; we may very well have perfected it now. All things are subjected to our perceptions of how we view ourselves and how we chose to let others define us. We can always do better or we can remain the same. The choice is ours. When it comes to personal relationships, it's no different. We attract what we feel about ourselves based on our level of confidence and insecurities. Women who experience high levels of self-esteem and have essentially addressed their personal issues are comfortable with who they are. They don't feel threatened by others opinions or attitudes although they may still carry their insecurities inside and are cautious with how they present themselves, not wanting to draw attention or rock the boat. There may be a number of feelings that arise when rejection happens and they will have to evaluate whether they want to be subjected to fears, embarrassment, isolation, sadness, disappointment, guilt, anger, and doubt.

We all have personal choices and we get to chose if we can do better or if we really want to. Try putting yourself in a place of quietness with no distractions, reviewing the whole situation, and asking yourself what would it have been like if this negative experience did not even occur? We have control over everything that concerns our intellectual facilities. Just because an event happened and we feel it is causing us to remain stagnant and traumatized in any way, we can choose to process the experience differently or seek out the help of professionally trained and experienced NLP Practitioners or Certified Life Coaches like myself who use methods with or without hypnosis to help clients shift effortlessly through non-desirable life events.

It's amazing how things are affected by emotional attachment. Once we release these dominate emotions and replace them with positive new perspectives, it changes the whole chemistry of our reactions. Our perceptions are powerful. Imagine looking out of a window from ground level to a group of people. Then envision looking out of another window from the 5th floor. Everything and everyone you were looking at is transformed. You can see things you couldn't earlier. You can visualize more and experience a completely different emotion, not from such a personal space, but from a broader and safer approach. You are not connected as you once were by just being focused on the fixed view you had from ground level. Do you see how the emotions changed? This is how it feels to detach negative emotions. It helps you to be in control of which perspective you would like to view and experience your memory from. You can always do better and perceive situations from a different perspective if you choose to see the benefits for yourself.

9. **What's stopping me from doing better?** Great! I'm so glad we are discussing this. I love to help people understand the plain and simple fact that no one else can make you happy if you don't want to be.

129

We are all accountable for our actions, reactions and overall behaviours. How others treat us is a combination of how we choose to view ourselves and what we tell others to treat us like. If we want to do better, many of us just do it without hesitation. If you are a procrastinator however, you are not alone and have nothing to be ashamed of. Everyone starts somewhere and the point of awareness is the beginning of real change.

As we already discussed goal setting in Chapter 12: *Goal Setting is Sexy!*, I would like to speak directly to those of you who are waiting for someone to get up and give them permission to take more control of their lives. You know exactly who you are and how you feel. You have carried this baggage around long enough and know why. It can only be taken care of by you. No man, woman, or child will ever take your baggage and deal with it no matter how much they love and care about you because everyone has their own baggage. It's just not possible for anyone to step inside your past experiences and re-live them for you to make you feel better about yourself. So sooner or later, you and only you will have to make a decision to do what is best and feel good about who you are!

You are fearfully and wonderfully made created in the image of God. You are a gift to this world and you are a beautiful creation. It doesn't matter where you came from, what you did in the past, or who did what to you. You are alive and kicking! You have a hope and a future and you get to create by your thoughts, prayers, dreams, and plans! You are a blessing to all who know you. You light up the room when you enter in. Your smile is like a bouquet of roses and you can make a grown man cry like a baby. How's that's for power? You and only you are meant to be the wonderful, beautiful you that you are.

I am so proud of you. The very fact that you are almost finished reading my book tells me that you really do love and care about making your life better. There is so much untapped potential inside of you just waiting to be released right now. Now it's time to give yourself the chance to be all you can be. You know the things you have dreamed of becoming and doing. It's time to step into your destiny. Be a blessing. Be the nice neighbour. Be the forgiving individual. You choose to let go of the nonsense and take control of your life. You are an amazing woman. Anything you did yesterday, you can do it better today. Choose to only compete with yourself as a way to motivate and strive higher. There is no losing with this perspective. You are a winner all the way.

Be a leader by example at work and offer your free time in the community. If you feel you don't have spare time, start making a schedule and plan new adventures into yours schedule. Complete unfinished projects. You have always been able to do better had you wanted to, but the awareness was not so prevalent and clear, and it held you back at times. As a nurse, I have witnessed individuals who did not have a second chance to make things better in their lives, whether it was with relationships, dreams, or goals. You can do this. You can do better and you can make the best of any situation if you really want to.

Absolutely You Keys for Empowerment #21

Never allow yourself to become bitter and harsh.
Every negative experience has its purpose.
If you can look past your pain deep within your heart,
It will stir up the positive energy towards others.
You are made of love and just as you like to be loved, so
do others.
You can overcome rejection with grace.

22 Jealousy is No Woman's Friend

Wow! I think I have saved the best one for last! How many women have had to deal with jealousy or maybe they were the jealous party? I think we can all agree that jealousy is probably the hottest unspoken topic in the airways right now. We've more than likely faced it growing up in the classrooms and school yards throughout the world, and we've all been on the receiving end of someone's envy or bad feelings.

Jealousy makes the most beautiful of hearts become indifferent and darkened. When you really examine resentful attitudes, why would anyone want to possess this negative destructive behaviour? Something so intolerable can only attract more of its negativity and envy into one's life. It would be like feeding a snake. Do you really think a snake would be satisfied with little morsels or would it get hungry for more? You see, the darkness of jealousy stems from low self-esteem because when someone is truly content with who they are, there is no fear of competition or upstaging.

Consider your own personal experiences. Were they pleasant or painfully uncomfortable? For myself, I have faced many situations where jealousy became quite obvious and caused me to have mixed feelings and heartache because of how it had taken me by surprise. I was not prepared to believe that people close to me would harbour such hurtful and awful emotions against me. Initially I didn't realize that it had nothing to do with me at all. In fact, as I went on to achieve more and more things in my life, it became quite prevalent how envious certain acquaintances really were. Honestly, how more obvious could it be when they would not even acknowledge my accomplishments but would have a celebration and announce throughout the community when it came to their own or their loved ones achievements.

The sting of jealousy from others has been difficult for my mom as she had to listen to many individuals boast. Yet those same people did not realize that both of my parents walked through cancer and survived, not knowing if they would even live to see their children become successful. My achievements have been motivated by my love for my children and my parents. I already know that my husband is very proud of me. For those of you who have something to say, I did not have a perfect marriage. I allowed too many people to stick their noses into my life, give their opinions and judge us when we really needed love and support.

After the loss of our daughter, you can imagine the grief and anxiety it caused. We did not have any extended family support and it was never mentioned by our relatives who were a large part of our social network. They may have talked behind our backs but never were we given the emotional help we needed.

Another time, I had a Pastor confirm to me that the people closest to me were so jealous and I should be aware of this. I then made a decision to step away from everyone who looked down at me and did not bring blessings into my life. It was obvious by they way they treated me, or talked to and about me. One of the things I will never forget was attending family functions as I could feel the heavy, choking energy that was around us. I knew that my family was being talked about and from observing the artificial attitude and smiles, there was no doubt we did not need to be around that atmosphere anymore. It was the best decision I had made in quite a while.

Jealousy surfaces during critical times of personal growth and development. I completed my training to become a specialized emergency room Trauma Nurse for different hospitals in the Ontario Golden Horseshoe. Imagine, I was that little brown girl whom no one believed in and had to encourage myself to be motivated and think that I was intelligent and worthy. Certain people were jealous when I had my mom baby-sit my 2 year old son while I completed my curriculum of nursing studies. I was forced to file a complaint with the Human Rights Commission against my former Nursing School for the racial, verbal and mental abuse I endured as a student with a perfect GPA of 4.0! I then enrolled with an online University and became an advanced level Certified Life Coach, completing all levels, and received training as a Business Consultant.

I have learned that jealousy is damaging to one's soul and steals the joys and happiness from one's life. I am content with who I am and this is who I choose to be. I am a very mindful person and have seen so many fallouts from envy. Women can get caught up so easily by the lies and false accusations of their peers and lose trust and respect. If only more women would realize that this jealousy nonsense will just end up coming back to them eventually. It will stir up negative garbage that will hurt someone and that pain will boomerang, causing heartache somewhere down the road. As a nurse I often wonder how much of this negativity is responsible for health issues that are so prevalent with women these days. Stress has been researched as one of the leading causes for illness and complications with women's health whether through career or personal experiences.

Why is it acceptable for certain people to receive an over abundance of love and support, yet when others accept any support whatsoever, it's an issue, seriously? Why is okay for some but not others? Jealousy has many facets and yet it has no face. You decide what you see and how you want to let it affect you.

I would like to tell you something very important. Everything you have right now, you have attracted into your life. So consider what it is you want, including friends, and continue loving and accepting everything about who you are. Stop being cynical and judgemental. Forgive yourself and choose to make yourself happy. I want to tell you three things my friend: you don't need to please anyone, you do not need to compete with anyone, and you don't have to be jealous of anyone. Your path in life is hard enough already.

I am so grateful to God for what he is doing through me and am appreciative of this journey. I don't have time for jealousy. Do you? Envy is everywhere and it will block your inspiration and motivation to move ahead. Many people have chosen to speak highly of their own and completely ignore my success. I don't care anymore. I'm not at that level. Life goes on. My mom and I often discuss why people can be so cruel and unkind. I've always encouraged my mom and told her how much I love her and dad and am so grateful for their love and support.

What those jealous individuals have failed to realize is that they are only hurting themselves and blocking their own success and happiness. They can use all the excuses they want. I could never understand their behaviours and actions, but as time has progressed I am determined to never let anyone get the best out of me or discourage my passion and purpose in life. I have consistently forgiven these individuals instead of holding onto the shock of their behaviours towards me. I placed them into a different category of my life because I learned that people will always reveal their motives to you one way or another. They may think they have the upper hand over you, belittle and use you, talk down about you or even out rightly discourage and verbally abuse you, but you don't have to own these things. You can choose to release it all and detach yourself from them emotionally.

Your energy does not need to be wasted trying to make others feel better about themselves. Imagine the irony in that? Someone chooses to dislike you and hate on you, yet you pour yourself all over them making them feel loved and valued while you're treated like a doormat. I've been there and done that. Then I realized how silly of me! These people don't care! What in the world am I doing!?

I can be respectful and kind and sincere. But I am no ones doormat! I am perfect the way I am and so are you! God has a plan for your life and it's time to let go of all the disappointments, jealousy, and garbage!

Jealousy is no woman's friend and it destroys too many relationships everyday. No one wants to talk about it but yet it's constantly happening everywhere. What's wrong with this picture?

I would love to speak to the jealous streak in all of us. We are human beings and we all like nice things. But truth be told, you don't know what anyone else went through to gain the status or notoriety they earned or to get the things they have in life. Why would anyone be jealous of someone else's difficulties in life?

I have been hurt by people I opened my heart to and let into my world. Those people were very close to me and had no remorse for the things they did. Why would I ever want what someone else has and attract their drama and negativity into my own life? For me personally, I don't have time wishing I had someone else's stuff. My stuff was hard earned as it is.

I have walked through rejection, jealousy, hate, racism, verbal, mental and physical abuse. I've endured many sleepless nights helping others who did not appreciate it and some couldn't even bother to speak or associate with me.

But, guess what? It doesn't bother me anymore because I know who I am. I am confident in myself. I am a better person for helping others whether they choose to appreciate it or not. I want blessings to come into my life and I choose peace, love, and forgiveness. It's better to love and not judge. Don't be jealous and forgive often.

I just can't understand how people who have such strong opinions of others could never humble themselves and realize that what they want for themselves, they should allow for others also.

Unfortunately, it's not until they experience the harsh effects of jealousy do they wake up. You don't really know what another person is living through. Can you feel their emotions and pain? That other woman might come from a broken home filled with loneliness and abuse. Is it really worth bringing someone else's energy into your world?

Choose to let go of any jealousy you may be feeling right at this moment. It's not you and honestly, do you really like how its making you feel inside? For those of you being traumatized by the pains of jealousy, I encourage you to please LET IT GO.

Forgive your offenders and release yourself from this prison of stress and grief. You don't deserve this and you are way better off changing your energy and focus. Remember, what you focus on becomes relevant and real in your world. Your dominant thoughts and emotions will manifest into your life. When you do shift into a higher level, if your friends or family change the way they treat you, were they really there for you to begin with? If you are inspired to become a better person and do more with your life, you will most certainly face some kind of opposition. This is the time you must stay more focused and positive. It's not easy. The road may be long and lonely because you will find not everyone wants to come around you to be that kind of friend you need. Some people will get strange and avoid you or stir up trouble to distract you on your path.

You may find the support that you thought was there has wandered away. You will have disrupted things around you by shifting your energy so there will be bumps along the way.

But don't give up! You can do it! People are uncomfortable when they see you working harder. They don't like to be shown up. Who cares! You are not responsible to make everyone feel good about themselves! For goodness sake, they can do that themselves.

You are important and jealousy is no woman's friend. Release it and let it go.

Absolutely You Keys for Empowerment #22

Every woman loves her friends.
Every friend loves to be loved.
Competition has no friends.
Jealousy is no woman's friend!

CONCLUSION

Thank you so much for taking the time to appreciate what I have to say about so many things that are very important to me.

I am grateful for each and every one of you and acknowledge that your lives are unique and special. I want you to be blessed and know how important you are to myself and your fellow sisters around the world.

Women are loving creatures and we are capable of so much love and affection. Yet many times we attack each other needlessly with no remorse. I don't want you to remain hurt and wounded. I want you to rise up and be the woman you were born to be. You know exactly who that is.

Think back and remember the dreams and goals you once had and held dear to your heart. It may be a while since you have acknowledged them. But, I want you to understand that no one can take them away from you if they are tucked away in your heart.

You see there is a time for everything in our lives. There is:
A season of grieving.
A season of releasing
A season of forgiving
A season of faith.
A season of healing
A season of love.
A season of renewal.
A season of new beginnings.
A season of happiness.
A season of enlightenment.

A season of growing.
A season of restoration.
A season of harvesting.
A season of reflection.

Through these seasons, we learn so much about ourselves and the lives we are living. We are always in control of our lives and we get to choose how we will respond to any given circumstance. There is no right or wrong way to live your life. There is no magic answer and no hidden meanings. Life is not a game; it is a journey of unlimited possibilities.

My hope for you my dear readers is that you will make the best of your life. Don't let the voices and opinions of others destroy your inner peace and happiness. It's so easy to let others steal your joy.

We can be content and satisfied in life while maintaining our peace and tranquility. When we remain in this state, life reveals so many opportunities for growth and enlightenment. We will easily attract exactly what we desire and need into our world. Things will shift effortlessly.

You are blossoming into the beautiful flower that you were created to be. Your children will call you blessed. Your mate will honour and support you.

Don't follow the crowd. You were born to stand out and nothing worth gaining in life is easy. You can do it! I believe in you and everything that you touch will prosper.

Bless those who hurt and speak badly of you. If it means releasing and moving on, do so eagerly. Do not hesitate when on the edge of your breakthrough. What you want, also wants you. You are the queen of your destiny and you can do this. When you are lonely, look up to the stars. Your creator made a magnificent universe and placed all of the stars so beautifully above to light the way in this dark and tedious world.

You are loved! Your true love will find you and when he does, you'll know exactly what to do. Remember, it's not all about you anymore. Life is about to get very exciting. Hold on and don't let go. This is what you've been waiting for and this is the right time.

You don't need to worry about idle talk and nonsense. You are more than that. You don't need to act uncivilized. You are a Queen and you are beautiful in all your ways.

As you choose to love yourself more, everyone around you will love you also. Give your love to those who need it. Be a blessing everywhere you go. Spread peace and watch what will start happening around you. The world will change right before your eyes.

Forgive more and allow the peace and tranquility of this whole big universe to pour out so much love and positivity onto your path. Every child wants to be loved. Give them what they need and let's heal the world one person at a time. God is love and you are created in the image of God.

Thank you for coming on this journey with me.

Dear God of the Universe, I pray a special blessing over each person who reads my words in this book. May it reach them at the perfect time. May it be well received and may they be blessed with the beauty of love in every area of their lives. Amen.

ABOUT THE AUTHOR

Anita Sechesky is a Registered Nurse, Life Coach, International Best-Selling Author, Keynote Speaker, Big Vision Consultant, and an NLP and LOA Practitioner. She has been a practicing RN for almost 10 years, gaining extensive knowledge and skills caring for people facing a variety of medical challenges in health care. She has worked in hospitals and nursing homes where she enjoys working with all client age groups. She is specialized in Trauma Nursing as an Emergency Room nurse.

Anita is also the best-selling author of several books in the anthology series *Living Without Limitations.*

As a Certified Life Coach, Anita has gained more clarity about her own passion of empowering others. Anita has mentored and coached people from the music and television industries, health care workers, entrepreneurs, social media, career transitions, Realtors, etc. She provides career coaching to new graduates entering the competitive job market, as well as resume and cover letter packages. Anita is the CEO and Owner of the company Anita Sechesky - Living Without Limitations. Her vision for her company is to empower and inspire others to live their lives without limitations such as false beliefs, grief, past failures, broken dreams, struggling relationships, finding your identity, lost hope, health conditions, lies, and labels placed on them by others.

In the past, Anita faced many things, which she had to find the strength and courage within herself to overcome. She has eagerly embraced opportunities of advancement that life presented, many times having to deal with the negativity or limitations placed on her by others. Anita recalls when she was a young girl growing up in a small community in North-western Ontario, Canada, that not everyone was nice, kind, or as supportive as she expected them to be. Anita eventually came to understand that this was the reality of a world of broken people. An individual cannot be expected to give love, compassion, empathy, kindness, or encouragement if they have not truly experienced unconditional love and acceptance themselves.

From the time Anita was a Grade Four student in Public School, she was determined become a Registered Nurse and help as many people as she could. As an adult, she achieved her dream, becoming a nurse after enduring much heartache and pain. Anita was an enthusiastic student with a GPA of 4.0, yet faced excessive harshness and rejection from people who she looked up to and respected. Sadly even the ones who were supposed to be her most loyal and supportive fans let her down in life because of jealousy, competition, or hatred. Anita learned that she cannot change anyone; she can only change herself.

From her traumatic experiences, Anita realized how powerful the human spirit truly is. She has always loved working on various medical floors, caring and communicating with all client age groups. Anita enjoys building resume and cover letters to empower those who are in transition with their careers.

She appreciates education and promotes continual learning as a form of life enhancement. One of Anita's favourite motivational quotes is: "Whatever your mind can conceive, you can achieve."

Please contact Anita at the following links:

Website: www.anitasechesky.com
FaceBook: www.facebook.com/AnitaSechesky
FaceBook Fan Page: www.facebook.com/asechesky
Twitter: @nursie4u
Skype: anita.sechesky
Email: asechesky@hotmail.ca
Linkedin: ca.linkedin.com/pub/anita-sechesky/3b/111/8b9
Pinterest: pinterest.com/anitasechesky

Manor House
905-648-2193

www.ingramcontent.com/pod-product-compliance
Lightning Source LLC
Chambersburg PA
CBHW032043040426
42334CB00038B/586